The Father

Letters to Sons and Daughters

Books by Evan Jones

The Father

* * *

Letters to Sons and Daughters

EDITED BY EVAN JONES

RINEHART & COMPANY, INC. *New York Toronto*

Published simultaneously in Canada by
Clarke, Irwin & Co., Ltd., Toronto

Copyright © 1960 by Evan Jones
Printed in the United States of America
Library of Congress Catalog Card Number: 60-6354

Acknowledgment

This book would have been impossible without the co-operation of many publishers and individuals to whom grateful acknowledgment is hereby made. In addition, special thanks are due the following persons for supplying valuable material and for heartening encouragement: Samuel Becker, Mrs. Elgar Blake, Suzanne Bloch, Mrs. Frederick Eberstadt, Donald Elder, Louis Fischer, Edward W. Forbes, Dagmar Godowsky, John Gunther, Thurman L. Hood, William A. Jackson, Horace H. F. Jayne, Judith Bailey Jones, John Lardner, S. M. Levitas, Sterling Lord, Mrs. Ivor Loving, Robert Mackworth-Young, Harry A. Maule, André Maurois, Leonard Meyberg, Ogden Nash, Justine Wise Polier, John Rewald, Cornelia Otis Skinner, Sylvia Sussman, Madame D. G. de Tinan, Alexandra Tolstoy, Pasteur Vallery-Radot, Marybeth Weston; Anne Wheaton, associate press secretary to President Eisenhower; W. L. White, William A. Wise.

Individual copyright credits follow:

Sherwood Anderson to his sons (two letters): *Letters of Sherwood Anderson,* edited by Howard Mumford Jones. Little, Brown & Co. Copyright 1953 Eleanor Anderson.

Audubon to his son: *Audubon the Naturalist,* by Francis A. Herrick. Copyright 1938 D. Appleton-Century Co., Inc.

Alexander Boswel to James Boswell: with permission of McGraw-Hill Book Co., Inc. from *Boswell in Holland 1763–1764,* edited by Frederick A. Pottle. Copyright 1928, 1952 Yale University.

General William Booth to his daughter: *Life of William Booth,* by Harold Begbie. Copyright 1920 Macmillan & Co., Ltd.

Robert Browning to his son: *Letters of Robert Browning.* Copyright 1933 Thurman L. Hood. Yale University Press.

John Clare to his son: *Letters of John Clare,* edited by J. W. and Anne Tibble. Routledge & Kegan Paul, Ltd.

Richard Harding Davis to his daughter: *Adventures and Letters of Richard Harding Davis,* edited by Charles Belmont Davis. Copyright 1917 Charles Scribner's Sons, renewal copyright 1945 Hope Harding Davis Kehrig.

Debussy to his daughter: *Lettres de Claude Debussy à Sa Femme Emma*, présentées par Pasteur Vallery-Radot. Copyright 1957 Ernest Flammarion.

Alexandre Dumas to his son and daughter (two letters): *The Titans*, by André Maurois. Harper & Brothers. Copyright 1957 André Maurois and used with his permission.

Edward Elgar to his daughter: *Letters of Edward Elgar*, edited by Percy M. Young. Geoffrey Bles Ltd. By permission of Mrs. Elgar Blake.

Ralph Waldo Emerson to his daughter: *Letters of Ralph Waldo Emerson*, edited by Ralph L. Rusk. Columbia University Press. Copyright 1939 Ralph Waldo Emerson Memorial Association.

Father in Communist China to his son: *Letters from the Communes*, by Richard L. Walker. *The New Leader*, June 15, 1959.

F. Scott Fitzgerald to his daughter: *The Crack-Up*, edited by Edmund Wilson. Copyright 1945 New Directions. Reprinted by permission of New Directions.

H. H. Furness to his son: *Letters of H. H. Furness*, edited by H. H. F. Jayne. Houghton Mifflin Co. By permission of Mr. Jayne.

Gandhi to his son: *Life of Gandhi*, by Louis Fischer. Harper & Brothers. Copyright 1950 Louis Fischer and used with his permission.

George V to Prince of Wales: *A King's Story*, by H.R.H. Edward, Duke of Windsor. Copyright 1947, 1950, 1951 H.R.H. Edward, Duke of Windsor. Published by G. P. Putnam's Sons. Used by permission.

George VI to Princess Elizabeth: *King George VI, His Life and Reign*, by John Wheeler-Bennett. Copyright 1958. St. Martin's Press. By permission of The Librarian, Windsor Castle.

John Hay to his daughter: *Life and Letters of John Hay*, edited by William Roscoe Thayer. Houghton Mifflin Co.

Sam Houston to his son: *The Writings of Sam Houston*, edited by Amelia W. Williams and Eugene C. Barker. University of Texas Press.

Robert G. Ingersoll to his daughter: *Letters of Robert G. Ingersoll*, edited by Eva I. Wakefield. Copyright 1951 Philosophical Library, Inc.

Henry James Sr. to Henry James: *Notes of a Son and Brother*, by Henry James. Copyright 1914 Charles Scribner's Sons; renewal copyright 1942 Henry James.

William James to his daughter: *Letters of William James*, edited by Henry James. Little, Brown & Co. Permission to reprint granted by Paul R. Reynolds & Son, 599 Fifth Avenue, New York.

James Joyce to his son and daughter-in-law: *Letters of James Joyce,* edited by Stuart Gilbert. Copyright 1957 Viking Press, Inc. and reprinted with their permission.

Robert A. Keyworth to his unborn child: *A Book of War Letters,* edited by Harry A. Maule. Copyright 1943 Random House, Inc.

Ring Lardner to his son: *Ring Lardner,* by Donald Elder. Doubleday, Inc. Copyright 1956 Donald Elder.

Six lines, *General William Booth Enters Into Heaven,* by Vachel Lindsay. Copyright 1923 Macmillan Co.

David Livingstone to his son: *Personal Life of David Livingstone,* by W. G. Blaikie. By permission John Murray Publishers Ltd.

George Meredith to his daughter: *Letters of George Meredith.* By permission Charles Scribner's Sons.

Leopold Mozart to his son: *Letters of Mozart and His Family,* edited by Emily Anderson. Published by Macmillan & Co., Ltd. and St. Martin's Press, Inc.

Ogden Nash to his daughter. By permission of Mr. Nash and Mrs. Frederick Eberstadt.

Louis Pasteur to his children: *La Correspondance de Pasteur.* By permission of Librarie Flammarion.

Camille Pissarro to his son: *Camille Pissarro—Lettres à Son Fils Lucien,* par John Rewald. Copyright 1950 Editions Albin Michel. By permission Mr. Rewald.

William Sidney Porter to his daughter: *O. Henry,* by C. Alphonso Smith. Doubleday, Page & Co.

Theodore Roosevelt to his sons (two letters): *Theodore Roosevelt's Letters to His Children,* edited by Joseph Bucklin Bishop. Copyright 1919 Charles Scribner's Sons; renewal copyright 1947 Edith K. Carow Roosevelt.

Dagobert D. Runes to his son: *Letters to My Son,* by Dagobert D. Runes. Copyright 1949 Philosophical Library, Inc.

Damon Runyon to his son: *Father's Footsteps,* by Damon Runyon, Jr. By permission Samuel Becker, Chase Manhattan Bank, Trustee, Estate of Damon Runyon.

Nicola Sacco to his son: *Letters of Sacco and Vanzetti,* edited by Marion Denman Frankfurter and Gardner Jackson. Copyright 1928, 1956 Viking Press, Inc. and reprinted with their permission.

Otis Skinner to his daughter (two letters): *Family Circle,* by Cornelia Otis Skinner. Houghton Mifflin Co. By permission Cornelia Otis Skinner.

For my children

"The Most Immediate Breath of Life . . ."

The father's heart may be as bold and errant as that of Dumas *père*, as weak and hurting as the soul of Edward II. Men learn to be fathers as they learn to live. They show what they have learned in many ways, but it is, perhaps, in letters that the male parent comes closer than in anything else to revealing his unprotected, undefensive self. No matter what he chooses to put on paper, a father's letter contains at least a glimpse of his love, and of his hope. That glimpse shines through the admonition or advice, and helps to reveal the individual and his time. Though he be sternly moral—in the manner of his era—between his lines there is a clue to what makes him so. Though he be gayly casual, he may not hide his anxious watchfulness. He may be proud, vain, superior, or admiring—in writing to his child he shows a quality of himself revealed in nothing else he writes. The purpose of this book is to offer something of the friendliness and wit and feeling, something of the concerns and moral attitudes, the ambitions and the dreams of men whose letters to their children have been preserved.

Once Goethe wrote, "We lay aside letters, never to read them again, and at last we destroy the most beautiful, the most immediate breath of life, irrevocably for ourselves and for others." And this is true. Yet how fortunate we are that so many letters have survived neglect and escaped destruction—and that enough of these are letters from men to their children, letters that throw new light on the greatness in a man by revealing him in his most fulfilling role—as the male parent.

"The joys of parents are secret," said Francis Bacon, "and so are their griefs and fears." Yet secret or unguarded, it is such emotions that give the letters of fathers special interest. "My hair stands on end at the costs and charges of these boys," Dickens once exploded to a friend. "Why was I ever a father! Why was my father ever a father!" He wrote in a moment of dire distraction, but he wrote honestly of what that temporary frustration made him feel.

The relationship with sons has concerned fathers throughout history. "There is something about the relationship that is pretty difficult to put your finger on." The words are Sherwood Anderson's in a letter to his son John. "I think fathers realize this and have it in their minds a good deal more than sons realize . . . It may be true of all relationships. . . . Nothing seems fixed. Everything is always changing. We seem to have very little control over our emotional life. . . ."

Fathers are not always so successful in carrying on discussions by mail. There is the cry, in the pages that follow, of the Restoration father who tells his son in college, "when I take a journey I always write unto my father by every opportunity . . . why I should be thus neglected by my son I cannot imagine . . ." Or there is to be remembered the admonishment in the correspondence between F. Scott Fitzgerald and his daughter: "You haven't answered a question for six letters. Better do so or I'll dock five dollars next week to show you I'm the same old meany." Or here in the sixteenth-century tones of Thomas More is the explicit exposition of what he thought a father has the right to expect from his children:

The Bristol merchant brought me your letters the day after he left you, with which I was extremely delighted. Nothing can come from your workshop, however rough and unfinished, that will not give me more pleasure than the most accurate thing anyone else can write. So much does my affection for you recommend whatever you write to me. Indeed, without any recommendation, your letters are capable of pleasing by their own merits, their wit and pure Latinity.

There was not one of your letters that did not please me

extremely; but to confess frankly what I feel, the letter of my son John pleased me most, both because it was longer than the others, and because he seems to have given it more labour and study. For he not only put out his matter prettily, and composed in fairly polished language, but he plays with me both pleasantly and cleverly, and turns my own jokes on myself prettily enough. And this he does not only merrily, but with due moderation, showing that he does not forget that he is joking with his father, and that he is careful not to give offence at the same time that he is eager to give delight.

Now I expect from each of you a letter almost every day. I will not admit excuses—John makes none—such as want of time, the sudden departure of the letter-carrier, or want of something to write about. No one hinders you from writing, but on the contrary, all are urging you to do it. And that you may not keep the letter-carrier waiting, why not anticipate his coming, and have your letters written and sealed, ready for anyone to take? How can a subject be wanting when you write to me, since I am glad to hear of your studies or of your games, and you will please me most if, when there is nothing to write about, you write about that nothing at great length! This must be easy for you, especially for the girls, who, to be sure, are born chatterboxes, and who have a world to say about nothing!

One thing however I admonish you: whether you write serious matters or the merest trifles, it is my wish that you write everything diligently and thoughtfully. It will be no harm if you first write the whole in English, for then you will not have much trouble in turning it into Latin; not having to look for the matter, your mind will be intent only on the language. That, however, I leave to your own choice, whereas I strictly enjoin you, that whatever you have composed, you carefully examine before writing it out clean, and in this examination first scrutinize the whole sentence, and then each part of it. Thus, if any solecisms have escaped you, you will easily detect them. Correct these, write out the whole letter again, and even examine it once more, for sometimes, in re-writing, faults slip in again that one had expunged. By this diligence, your little trifles will become serious matters, for while there is nothing so neat and witty that may not be made insipid by silly and inconsiderate chatter, so also there is nothing in itself so insipid, that you cannot season it with grace and wit if you give a little thought to it.

Farewell, my dear children.

When, in this letter, Sir Thomas assures his children that "you will please me most if, when there is nothing to write about, you write about that nothing at great length," he is paraphrasing the appeal that Pliny the Younger made fourteen centuries earlier: "You say there is nothing to write about. Then write to me that there is nothing to write about." For fathers, like all other letter writers, want most of all to find through the mails a reaction to their own sense of being alive. "In a man's letters—" as Dr. Johnson said "—his soul lies naked." In his letters to his children he shows a deeper self.

In this collection we find Samuel Taylor Coleridge enjoining a seven-year-old son to always tell the truth "both for its own sake, and because [your] dear Father . . . wrote so . . ." We find advice of all kinds, appeals of all kinds. Here we find Jack London accusing his former wife of sacrificing the future of his children, and discover that years later his daughter Joan believed it was through letters—even though London's family was irrevocably separated—"that father and daughters finally came to know each other." Here Nicolo Sacco writes from the death house to his thirteen-year-old boy, "Son, instead of crying, be strong, so as to be able to comfort your mother . . . love and be nearest your mother . . ." The words are an old echo of the fatherly heart: The Duke of Suffolk charges his son, "as ye be bounden by the commandment of God to do, to love, to worship, your lady and mother." In another vein, David Livingstone tells his son not to count on his influence because he has "little else than what people call a great name to bequeath . . ." Heinrich Schliemann, on the other hand, cannot understand why his child is not as arrogantly successful as himself. The unlucky Charles I urges his heir to be Charles *le bon* rather than Charles *le grand*.

It was the nineteenth-century critic, Sir Walter Raleigh, who said, "The chief interest of a study of the great letter writers is that it introduces us not to literary works, but to persons." In this collection the emphasis is on the letters that make men persons— some of them great men, some of them great letter writers, some of them great fathers only. These are intimate letters, not often concerned with turning points of history, and they have been brought together to show the myriad facets of fatherhood.

There may be some unfairness in the fact that letters which achieve durable form are most often those of fathers whose lives have been influential enough to bring them to the attention of biographers and other collectors of addenda. Certain it is that letters of warmth and beauty, or of wisdom or charm, are being treasured today—are being written today—in homes never to be searched by literary executors. It isn't hard to find an example:

"When life is given to a child, a ticket saying, 'one-way travel only,' is issued to him for his entire life. As he grows up and begins to live his own life, he examines the ticket for information as to how to begin his travels. Then he discovers his first problem. Not one word is written down; the ticket is blank. The answer is —only one road for all and each must decide for himself how he intends to travel. Now, Sylvia, you have a full life to go yet. Please take my advice . . . be careful in your going. Don't try to go too fast. You cannot make this trip twice. Don't look back, be-cause everyone is going one way and there is no return. Some-times the road is rough. Then you should take time out until it clears up."

In this advice from an unsung parent to an unsung child, the value is as instantly recognizable as in any words of men whose names may shine for a thousand years. For the Sylvia of the letter, the value is incomparable: "Happily, I never destroyed it, and when the going gets rough, as he said it would, I take it out and re-read it, still able to benefit from his courageous philosophy."

A letter provides the most personal form in which words may be used with lasting effect on paper. "Only on paper—" and the words are Bernard Shaw's "—has humanity yet achieved glory, beauty, truth, knowledge, virtue, and abiding love."

Thus in his letters a father finds the great challenge of his role—in this he is not merely consort to his child's mother; he is not merely the momentary disciplinarian, the wielder of symbolic switches; not merely the good companion. In fatherly letters he cannot wholly disguise himself.

Contents

I THE ROOTS OF LIVING

Count Castiglione Asks His Children for Reverence   3
Martin Luther Addresses a Parable to His Small Son   5
Sir William Penn Orders Home His Quaker Son   7
A Son Goes Off to College and Fails to Write His Father   9
Jefferson Prescribes a Routine for His Daughter   11
Coleridge Tells a Seven-Year-Old How Much He Is Missed   14
William Hazlitt Prescribes for a Son's Behavior at School   17
Andrew Jackson Hopes to Reform His Profligate Son   21
William James Analyzes a Daughter's Emotional Problems   22
Theodore Roosevelt Reviews His Son's Year at School   26
Gandhi Defines His Creed for Education   27
Nehru Sends a Present from Prison to His Daughter   31
Leopold Godowsky Leaves His Daughter in Europe   33
Scott Fitzgerald Writes a List of Do's and Don'ts   35
A Soldier's Letter to His Unborn Child   37

II FAMILY CIRCLE

Edward II Asks His Son to Disown His Mother's Infidelity   43
Oliver Cromwell Offers His Successor Some Advice   46
James II Beseeches His Daughter's Loyalty   48
Boswell Is Summoned Home from Europe on His Mother's
     Death   50
Franklin Discusses Death with His Daughter   52
Dumas *Père* Accuses His Son of Disregarding His Mistress
     and Dismisses the Criticism of His Daughter   54
Bronson Alcott Describes the Originals of *Little Women*   59

Daniel Webster Announces the Death of a Son in War   *61*
Prince Albert Tells a Daughter What Her Marriage Means   *62*
Emerson Reacts to Becoming a Grandfather   *65*
George Meredith Sends a Chiding Rhyme   *66*
Tolstoy Turns a Daughter's Mind to Some Marital Problems   *67*
John Burroughs Entreats His Son to Marry Before He Is
    Twenty-four   *69*
Mark Twain Writes in Anguish After a Daughter's Death   *70*
Walter Hines Page Sizes Up His Loss, His Daughter's Gain   *71*
Jack London Makes a Last Ditch Stand for His Children   *73*
Rabbi Stephen Wise Celebrates His Fiftieth Year in America   *75*
George VI Tells How He Felt at Elizabeth's Wedding   *76*

III   THE GREAT WORLD

A Roman Bishop Urges His Son to Avoid Evil Company   *81*
A Banished Duke Says Good-bye to an Eight-Year-Old Heir   *85*
A Father's Letter Intercepted in Mary Stuart's Prison   *88*
Raleigh Tells His Son to Be Cautious in Friendship   *90*
Charles I Gives His Creed of Kingship to Charles II   *91*
Catherine the Great Is Instructed in Wifely Behavior   *96*
Diderot, in Prison, Reads a Lecture from His Father and De-
    scribes a Prescription to His Daughter   *98*
Lord Chesterfield Discusses a Few Rules of Business   *102*
Leopold Mozart Takes His *Wunderkind* to Task   *104*
Fanny Burney Is Urged to Reject M. D'Arblay   *106*
Walter Scott Has Some Thrifty Words for a Soldier Son   *110*
A Nineteenth Century Father Considers the Hazards of a
    Debut   *112*
Noah Webster Finds Fault with a White House Dinner   *114*
Coventry Patmore Gets His Father's Advice on Writing   *116*
Sam Houston Instructs a Soldier in His Duty to Texas   *119*
Dickens Sends His Youngest Son into the World of Men   *121*
Dr. Livingstone Describes the Heart of Africa   *124*
George V Sympathizes with the Prince of Wales   *130*

Sherwood Anderson Looks at His Generation's Influence 132
A Composer's Comments on the British Scene 137
William Allen White Carries Prohibition Abroad 140
William Carlos Williams Considers His Son's Future 142
Ogden Nash Reacts to an Affair of a Foolish Heart 144
Damon Runyon Writes a Temperance Letter 146
Dagobert Runes Points Out the Problems of Being a Jew 150

IV HERITAGE AND THE HELPING HAND

Lorenzo the Magnificent Instructs a Future Pope 157
Audubon Invites a Son to Become His Assistant 162
Mendelssohn's Father Offers Some Criticism of *Ave Maria* 164
Heinrich Schliemann Spurs a Son to Emulate Himself 168
Henry James Is Offered Some Fatherly Help 170
H. H. Furness Points to the Artistry of Charlotte Brontë 174
Camille Pissarro Encourages a Painter Son 175
Sherwood Anderson Compares the Arts of Writing and Painting 177

V OCCASIONS OF MOMENT

Thomas More Addresses His Last Letter to His Daughter 183
Paul Revere, After His Midnight Ride, Writes to His Son 185
Horatio Nelson Receives His Father's Congratulations 186
Goethe Writes to His Son on the Day After a Great Battle 187
John Clare Asks His Sixteen-Year-Old Son for Freedom 189
James Fenimore Cooper Cheers a Literary Debut 191
John Brown Urges His Family to Abhor Slavery 193
Lee Reports on His Return to a Scene of Battle 197
Louis Pasteur Announces a Great Discovery 198
Trollope Cheers His Son's Election to an Exclusive Club 200
Robert Browning Applauds His Son's Good Fortune 203
John Hay Sketches a Moment of American History 205

General Booth Gives Thanks for Letters on His Blindness   *206*
Nicola Sacco Speaks to His Son As He Faces Execution   *209*
Ernest Bloch Discusses the Effects of World War II   *214*
General Eisenhower Writes a Letter from a Sicilian Tunnel   *218*
A Father in Communist China Writes a Son Who Has
    Escaped   *219*

VI THE LIGHT TOUCH

Lord Burghley Dips His Pen in Dubious Rhyme   *225*
Sir Richard Steele Takes Pleasure in Conversing   *226*
Sydney Smith Jokes with a Traveling Daughter   *227*
Victor Hugo Describes His Travels to His Children   *229*
The 'Father of *Little Women*' to the 'Mother of *Little Men*'   *231*
Thackeray Sends an Illustrated Newsletter   *233*
Bret Harte Writes of Some European Customs   *235*
T. H. Huxley Jests About the Departure of a Daughter   *239*
Robert G. Ingersoll Celebrates a Birthday   *240*
O. Henry Sends a Fairy Tale from Prison   *241*
Sir Edward Elgar Feeds His Daughter's Rabbits   *243*
Theodore Roosevelt Reports a Hunting Incident   *244*
Otis Skinner Brightens the Path for Cornelia Otis Skinner   *247*
Debussy Chats by Mail with His Eight-Year-Old Daughter   *250*
Richard Harding Davis Writes to a Baby Nine Months Old   *251*
Ring Lardner Rhymes an Appeal for Mail   *253*
James Joyce Merrily Chides His Son and Daughter-in-Law   *258*

Index   *261*

I

* * *

The Roots of Living

The father finds his role
before his child is born . . . and the meanings
of his child's future turn him to the roots
of living . . . respect for one's elders . . .
virtue . . . duty . . . discipline . . .
schooling the mind . . . cherishing health . . .
separating right from wrong . . .

And he shall turn
the heart of the fathers
to the children,
and the heart of the children
to the fathers . . .

Malachi iv, 6

Count Castiglione Asks His Children
for Reverence:

The Renaissance was in its apogee when Count Baldassare Castiglione, papal nuncio and Bishop of Avilla, wrote *Il Cortegiano,* one of the great books of sixteenth-century prose, referred to by Italians as *Il Libro d'oro.* Deeply involved in his career though he was, Castiglione was a devoted parent. He had lost his wife almost immediately after the birth of their third child, and his offspring were living with his mother in Mantua, since the count was kept much of the time with the Court of Charles V in Northern Spain. Even this distance did not diminish Castiglione's fatherly concern. The following letter of strict advice to his children was written in Latin for the benefit of his son Camillo, who was twelve, and the two girls, ten and eight.

To My Dearest Children, Camillo, Anna, and Ippolita.

I am sure, my dearest son Camillo, that you, above all things desire my speedy return home. For it is ordained, alike by Nature and the laws of man, that we reverence our parents next to God. And you may be said to owe me a special debt, since I have remained content with one son, and have been unwilling to share either my fortune or my love with another. You are bound, therefore, to pay me this filial duty, lest I should repent my resolution. And, although I have no doubt that you recognize this, I wish you to understand that I do not regard this duty lightly, as other parents often do, but I exact it from you as my due. This debt you will best discharge by looking upon the admirable teacher whom your friends have given you, in the light of a father, and by obeying his voice as if it were my own. I can give you no better advice than this line of Virgil, which I repeat in no boastful spirit:

> "Disce, puer, virtutem ex me, verumque laborem;
> Fortunam ex aliis."
> ["Learn, boy, from me, virtue and honorable toil;
> but good fortune from others."]

My Anna, who first taught me to use the sweet name of daughter, may your character be adorned with such moral graces that the beauties of your person may be excelled by that of your soul, and may be justly celebrated by posterity. And you, my Ippolita, whom I love so much, for the sake of her whose name you bear, how pleasant it would be if, in the practice of virtue, you could surpass your sister who is so much your elder in years! But go on, both of you, as you have begun, and imitate the pattern held up before your eyes by her who has nurtured you since your mother died, when you were too young to mourn her loss, so that all may with one voice exclaim how close a likeness you bear to her. Farewell.

Your father,
Baldassare Castiglione

Monzone, July 11, 1528.

Baldassare was dead in less than a year. With his advice, Camillo Castiglione entered the service of Charles V when he was seventeen, becoming general of the Mantuan armies and governor of Montferrato. He so conducted himself that he is considered by historians as a model of chivalry and virtue.

* * *

4

Martin Luther Addresses a Parable to His Small Son Hans:

Under the sweeping influence of the Reformation he had touched off, Martin Luther came to defend the breaking of monastic vows and the marriage of priests, arguing that celibacy had been invented by the Devil as a source of sin. Yet he himself was slow to marry. Four years after he wrote that the sexual impulse was both natural and irrepressible, he urged a group of nuns to leave their convent, and volunteered to find them husbands. When the engagement he arranged for Catherine von Bora failed to come off and the former nun was forced to find work as a domestic, he interpreted her plight as a threat from the Devil against himself. He married Catherine to spite the Devil. After so singular a persuasion, there is little surprise in the fact that Luther's acceptance of marriage had its ups and downs. By and large, however, it was an agreeable relationship in which Catherine ran her husband's farm and bore him six children, among whom was the son to whom Luther wrote the guileful appeal below.

[Coburg]

To my dear son, Hans Luther: Grace and peace in Christ, my darling little Son. I am very glad to hear that you are studying well and praying diligently. Go on doing so, my little son, and when I come home I will bring you a beautiful present.

I know a lovely, pretty garden, where there are many children. They wear golden coats, and pick up fine apples, pears, cherries, and plums under the trees. They sing and jump and are very merry. They also have little horses with bridles of gold and saddles of silver. I asked the man who owned the garden who the children were. He answered, "These are the

5

children who gladly pray and study and are good." Then I said, "Dear man, I also have a son named Hans Luther. Wouldn't he like to come into the garden and eat such beautiful apples and pears and ride such fine horses and play with these children!" Then the man said, "If he prays and studies gladly, and is good, he too shall come into the garden, and Lippus and Jost with him. And when they are all here they shall have whistles and drums and lutes and all sorts of things to make music with, and they shall dance and shoot with little crossbows." And he showed me a beautiful meadow in the garden fixed for dancing. Gold whistles were hung there, and drums and silver crossbows. But it was still early and the children had not yet eaten, so I couldn't wait for the dance, and I said to the man: "Dear sir, I will go as fast as I can and write it all to my dear son Hans, that he may study and pray well and be good and so come into this garden. But he has an Aunt Lena whom he will have to bring with him." Then the man said, "Very well, go and write to him."

Therefore, dear little son Hans, study and pray bravely, and tell Lippus and Jost to do so too, and you shall all come into the garden with each other. The dear God take care of you. Greet Aunty Lena and give her a kiss for me.

Your loving father,
Martin Luther

April 22, 1530

Luther loved his children and his wife, and he believed that women should devote themselves to bearing offspring and attending to their husbands' comforts. But he had some misgivings about procreation. In his *Table-Talk* he wrote, "Had God consulted me about it, I should have advised Him to continue the generation

6

of the species by fashioning human beings out of clay, as Adam was made."

* * *

"The cause of this writing
is to charge you . . ."

Sir William Penn Orders Home His Quaker Son Before Disowning Him:

A professional naval commander who served the Stuarts as well as Cromwell, William Penn the elder was not equipped to understand his son's sympathy for the Society of Friends. Sir William had raised his namesake as both a Puritan and a Cavalier; a gentleman commoner was not expected to have anything but scorn for the Quakers. When the son was arrested at a Quaker meeting in Cork, the news traveled fast to Sir William in London, and the father immediately sought his heir's return. It took several letters to bring the reunion about.

Navy Office, October 12, 1667

Son William:

I have writ several letters to you since I received any from you. By this I again charge you and strictly command that you come to me with all possible speed. In expectation of your compliance, I remain

Your affectionate father,
W. Penn

7

Another ten days passed.

Navy Office, October 22, 1667

Son William:

I hope this will find you in health. The cause of this writing is to charge you to repair to me with all possible speed, presently after your receipt of it, and not to make any stay there, or any place upon your road, until it pleases God you see me (unless for necessary rest and refreshment).

Your very affectionate father,
W. Penn

Young William Penn came—reluctantly; father and son argued futilely. At one point Sir William announced in a tremulous voice that he was going to kneel down and pray that his son be saved from becoming a Quaker. The young man's response was to fling open a casement and declare he would throw himself out before his father could pray for such a blasphemy. They were at loggerheads, and a year passed in uneasy truce. William was arrested again, and the magistrate notified the father directly that his son was consorting with Quakers. This time Sir William told his son to pack his bags and remove himself from his father's house; he would, the irate parent said, dispose of his estates "to them that pleased him better."

✳   ✳   ✳

A Son Goes Off to College and Fails to Write His Father:

The Civil War in England disturbed the lives of rich and poor alike, including the distinguished Verney family. The fortunes of Charles I brought exile and poverty to Sir Ralph Verney, and his son Edmund, as a result, was cheated of a college education. With the Stuarts back in power, however, Edmund saw to it that his own son was duly accepted at Oxford. The younger Edmund Verney seems to have been less enthusiastic about matriculation than his father.

London, 22 January, 1685

Child,

    I shall be very joyful to hear of your safe arrival at Oxford, according to my kind wishes which attended you all the way for your prosperous journey.

    I have this day sent you (by Thomas Moore the Oxon carrier) all your things mentioned in this enclosed note, except your old camelot coat, which I did not think you would need nor worth sending; your old hat I did not send neither, for it is so bad that I was ashamed of it. All your new things I bought you I put into a new box locked up and well corded up, and the key of this box I have also here-enclosed for you. But for the key of your trunk I could not find it, and it's no matter, for that lock is nothing worth, and Tom made a shift to lock it with a key of mine, and it is well corded besides.

    In your old breeches which are in your new box, you will find your five laced bands (the sixth you carried with you) and a new pair of laced cuffs, and your two guineas in your fob, and a

9

new knife and fork in your great pocket. And so God bless you, and send you well to do.

> I am your loving father,
> Edmund Verney

In your trunk I have put for you
  18 Seville oranges
  6 Malaga lemons
  3 pounds of brown sugar
  1 pound of white powdered sugar made up in quarters
  1 lb of brown sugar candy
  ¼ of a lb of white sugar candy
  1 lb of picked raisins, good for a cough
  4 nutmegs

When a week passed without a word—of thanks or anything else —Father Verney was vexed indeed.

29 January, 1685

Child,

Mr. Palmer had a letter from his son at Oxford last Saturday morning very early, and my cousin Denton Nicholas wrote to his parents from Wycombe and again from Oxford since his last arrival. And when I take a journey I always write unto my father by every opportunity a perfect diurnal of my voyage and what else occurs worthy of remark. I writ to you a letter this day seven-night when I sent your trunk and box, but never had any answer nor account from you since, which is such a piece of omission in you, to say no worse, that I believe neither Oxford nor Cambridge can parallel. For why I should be thus neglected by my son I cannot imagine: indeed I look upon it as an ill omen, that you should commit such a gross solecism at your first entrance into the University against your loving father

The following year, Edmund Verney, Jr., was guilty of another solecism. His father received a complaint from the boy's tutor about his cutting classes, and promptly demanded an explanation "by the next post."

*   *   *

*"I have placed my happiness
on seeing you good . . ."*

Jefferson Prescribes a Routine for His Motherless Daughter:

Fourteen months before this letter was written, Jefferson lost the wife with whom he had lived "ten years in unchequered happiness." Martha Jefferson's death, he said, left him in a "stupor of mind which had rendered me as dead to the world as she whose loss occasioned it;" for a year he virtually ceased writing letters. But in 1783 he was appointed a delegate to the Confederation Congress, and he placed his eldest daughter in a Philadelphia school. The long correspondence with his children, which he maintained whenever he was separated from them, begins with this letter to the eleven-year-old Patsy.

Dear Patsy,—After four days' journey, I arrived here without any accident, and in as good health as when I left Philadelphia. The conviction that you would be more improved in the situation I have placed you than if still with me, has solaced me on my parting with you, which my love for you has rendered a difficult thing. The acquirements which I hope you will make under the tutors I have provided for you will render you more worthy of my love; and if they cannot increase it, they will prevent its dimunition. Consider the good lady who has taken you under her roof, who has undertaken to see that you perform all your exercises, and to admonish you in all those wanderings from what is right and what is clever, to which your inexperience would expose you: consider her, I say, as your mother, as the only person to whom, since the loss with which Heaven has pleased to afflict you, you can now look up; and that her displeasure or disapprobation, on any occasion, will be an immense misfortune, which should you be so unhappy as to incur by any unguarded act, think no concession too much to regain her good will. With respect to the distribution of your time, the following is what I should approve:

From 8 to 10, practice music.

From 10 to 1, dance on one day and draw another.

From 1 to 2, draw on the day you dance, and write a letter next day.

From 3 to 4, read French.

From 4 to 5, exercise yourself in music.

From 5 to bedtime, read English, write, etc.

Communicate this plan to Mrs. Hopkinson, and if she approves of it, pursue it. As long as Mrs. Trist remains in Philadelphia, cultivate her affection. She has been a valuable friend to you, and her good sense and good heart make her valued by all who know her, and by nobody on earth more than me. I expect you to write me every day by post. Inform me what books you read, what tunes you learn, and enclose me your best copy of every lesson in drawing. Write also one letter a week either to your Aunt Eppes, your Aunt Skipworth, your Aunt Carr, or the little lady from whom I now enclose a letter, and always put the letter you so write under cover to me. Take care that you never spell a word wrong. Always before you write a word, consider how it is spelt, and, if you do not remember it, turn to a dictionary. It produces great praise to a lady to spell well. I have placed my happiness on seeing you good and accomplished; and no distress this world can now bring on me would equal that of your disappointing my hopes. If you love me, then strive to be good under every situation and to all living creatures, and to acquire those accomplishments which I have put in your power, and which will go far towards ensuring you the warmest love of your affectionate father.

P. S. Keep my letters and read them at times, that you may always have present in your mind those things which will endear you to me.

Here is a letter so restrained in showing emotion—so far removed from the twentieth-century attitudes of permissive parents—that it dims the picture of Jefferson as a very human father. Patsy recalled years later that he fainted after her mother's death "and remained so long insensible that they feared he would never revive. He kept his room three weeks and I was never a moment from his side." The rapport between this father and daughter was strengthened by loss. Death claimed five of the six children, leaving the President and Patsy, who had married Thomas

Randolph, as the only surviving Jeffersons. In one of the very last of his letters he called her "my dear and beloved daughter, the cherished companion of my early life, and the nurse of my age."

*   *   *

". . . you are a big Thought . . ."

Samuel Taylor Coleridge to His Seven-Year-Old Son Derwent:

Few have ever given more freely of themselves in their letters than did Coleridge. Hounded though he was by poor health, the consequent addiction to opium and the infelicity of his marriage, his separations from his children brought him misery. "Oh my children!" he wrote to his wife from Sicily. "I cannot write their names. Even to speak of them, there is an effort of courage." When he was with them, he described them joyfully to friends. When Derwent was three and his brother Hartley seven, Coleridge wrote Matthew Coates, *"Derwent* is a large, fat, beautiful child, quite the *pride* of the village, as Hartley is the *darling.* [Robert] Southey says wickedly that 'all Hartley's guts are in his brains, and all Derwent's brains are in his guts.' " When the younger boy was twelve, his father described him as "the self-same, fond, small, Samuel Taylor Coleridge as ever." Derwent was named after the river in Cumberland County, "for fronting our house the Greta runs into the Derwent." Coleridge had gone with Hartley to visit Wordsworth and the latter's sister Dorothy when he wrote this moving letter to his second son, aged seven.

My dear Derwent,

It will be many times the number of years, you have already lived, before you can know and feel thoroughly, how very much your dear Father wishes and longs to have you on his knees, and in his arms. Your Brother, Hartley, too whirls about, and wrings his hands at the thought of meeting you again: he counts the days and hours, and makes sums of arithmetic of the time, when he is again to play with you, and your sweet squirrel of a Sister. He dreams of you, and has more than once hugged me between sleeping and waking, fancying it to be you or Sara: and he talks of you before his eyes are fully open in the morning, and while he is closing them at night. And this is very right: for nothing can be more pleasing to God Almighty and to all good people, than that Brothers and Sisters should love each other, and try to make each other happy; but it is impossible to be happy without being good, and the beginning and the A.B.C. of goodness is to be dutiful and affectionate to their Parents; to be obedient to them, when they are present, and to pray for them, [and to write] frequent letters from a thankful and loving heart when both or either of them chance to be absent. For you are a big Thought, and take up a great deal of room in your Father's Heart: and his eyes are often full of tears thro' his Love of you, and his Forehead wrinkled from the labor of his Brain, planning to make you good, and wise and happy. And your *Mother* has fed and cloathed and taught you, day after day, all your life; and has passed many sleepless nights, watching and lulling you, when you were sick and helpless, and she gave *you* nourishment out of her own Breasts for so long a time, that the moon was at its least and its greatest sixteen times before you

15

lived entirely on any other food, than what came out of her body, and she brought you into the world with shocking Pains, which she suffered for you, and before you were born for eight months together every drop of blood in your body, first beat in *her* Pulses and throbbed in *her* Heart. So it must needs be a horribly wicked thing ever to forget, or wilfully to vex a Father or a Mother, especially a Mother. God is above all: and only good and dutiful children can say their Lord's Prayer, and say to God, *"our Father,"* without being wicked even in their Prayers. But after God's name, the name of Mother is the sweetest and most holy. The next good thing and that without which you cannot either honor any person, or be esteemed by anyone, is *always to tell the truth.* For God gave you a Tongue to tell the Truth, and to tell a Lie with it is as silly, as to try to walk on your Head instead of your Feet; besides it is such a base, hateful, and wicked thing, that when good men describe all wickedness put together in one wicked mind, they call it the Devil, which is Greek for *malicious Liar:* and the Bible names him a *Liar* from the beginning, and the Father of *Lies.* Never, never tell a Lie—even tho' you should escape a whipping by it; for the pain of a whipping does not last above a few minutes, and the Thought of having told a Lie would make you miserable for days—unless, indeed, you are hardened in wickedness and then you must be miserable for ever——

But you are a dear Boy, and will scorn such a vile thing: and whenever you happen to do anything amiss, which *will* happen now and then, you will say to yourself "Well whatever comes of it, I will *tell the Truth,* both for its own sake, and because my dear Father [spoke] and wrote so to me about it."

I am greatly delighted that you are desirous to go on with your Greek; and shall finish this letter with a short Lesson of

16

Greek. But more cannot be done till we meet, when we will begin anew, and, I trust, not to leave off, till you are a good scholar. And now go, and give a loving kiss to your little sister and tell her, that Papa sent it to her: and will give hundreds in a little time: for I am, my dear Child,

Your affectionate Father
S. T. Coleridge

P. S.   I find that I cannot write in this space what I wished— therefore I will send you, dear child! a whole sheet of Greek Lessons in a few days . . .

Derwent Coleridge became a distinguished scholar and author, the father of Christabel Coleridge, the novelist, and E. H. Coleridge, the critic and biographer. After Hartley's death in 1849, Derwent wrote a memoir of his brother, published with the latter's *Poems*. Derwent himself, his father wrote, had "very fine talents; and a particularly fine sense of metrical music. His lyric *Fantasies* are among the most musical schemes or movements in Verse, that I have ever met with . . ."

✳   ✳   ✳

"You are not . . . a king's son . . ."

William Hazlitt Prescribes for a Son's Behavior at School:

Respected though he was as a critic, Hazlitt was a man of such unpredictable and irascible temperament that he discouraged many friends. He was unable to make his marriage to Sarah Stoddart work, and in 1822, after falling in love with his land-lord's daughter, he divorced his wife and sent his son William to school. Though one of his friends called him "of all mortals the most open to ridicule," Hazlitt was able to muster some sound and not unconventional advice for the eleven-year-old boy who was reluctant to leave the security of family life.

[1822]

My Dear Little Fellow,

You are now going to settle at school, and may consider this as your first entrance into the world. As my health is so in-different, and I may not be with you long, I wish to leave you some advice (the best I can) for your conduct in life, both that it may be of use to you, and as something to remember me by. I may at least be able to caution you against my own errors, if nothing else.

As we went along to your new place of destination, you often repeated to me that you durst say that they were a set of stupid, disagreeable people at the school. You were to blame in this. It is a good rule to hope for the best. Always, my dear, be-lieve things to be right till you find them to the contrary; and even then, instead of irritating yourself against them, endeavour to put up with them as well as you can, if you cannot alter them. You said you were sure you would not like the school where you were going. This was wrong. What you meant was that you did not like to leave home. But you could not tell whether you should like the school or not, till you had given it a trial. Other-wise, your saying that you should not like it was determining that you would not like it. Never anticipate evils; or because you cannot have things exactly as you wish, make them out worse than they are, through mere spite and wilfulness.

You seemed at first to take no notice of your school-fellows, or rather to set yourself against them, because they were strangers to you. They knew as little of you as you did of them; so that this would have been a reason for their keeping aloof from you as well, which you would have felt as a hardship. Learn never to conceive a prejudice against others because you know nothing of them. It is bad reasoning, and makes enemies of half the world. Do not think ill of them till they behave ill to you; and then strive to avoid the faults which you see in them. This will disarm their hostility sooner than pique or resentment or complaint.

I thought you were disposed to criticise the dress of some of the boys as not so good as your own. Never despise any one for anything that he cannot help—least of all, for his poverty. I would wish you to keep up appearance yourself as a defence against the idle sneers of the world, but I would not have you value yourself upon them. I hope you will neither be dupe nor victim of vulgar prejudices. Instead of saying above, 'Never despise any one for anything he cannot help,' I might have said, 'Never despise any one at all'; for contempt implies a triumph over and pleasure in the ill of another. It means that you are glad and congratulate yourself on their failings or misfortunes.

You complain since, that the boys laugh at you and do not care about you, and that you are not treated as you were at home. My dear, that is one chief reason for you being sent to school, to inure you betimes to the unavoidable rubs and uncertain reception you may meet with in life. You cannot always be with me, and perhaps it is as well that you cannot. But you must not expect others to show the same concern about you as I should. You have hitherto been a spoiled child, and have been used to have your own way a good deal both in the house and among your play-fellows, with whom you were too fond of being a leader; but you have good-nature and good sense, and will get the better of this in time. You have now got among other boys who are your equals, or bigger and stronger than yourself, and who have something else to attend to besides humouring your whims and fancies, and you feel this as a repulse or piece of injustice. But the first lesson to learn is that there are other people in the world besides yourself.

There are a number of boys in the school where you are, whose amusements and pursuits (whatever they may be) are and ought to be of as much consequence to them as yours can be to you, and to which therefore you must give way in your turn. The more airs of childish self-importance you give yourself, you will only expose yourself to be the more thwarted and the more laughed at. True equality is the only true morality or true wisdom. Remember always that you are but one among others, and you can hardly mistake your place in society. In your father's house you might do as you pleased: in the world you will find competitors at every turn. You are not born a king's son, to destroy or dictate to millions; you can only expect to share their fate, or settle their differences amicably with them. You already find it so at school, and I wish you to be reconciled to your situation as soon and with as little pain as you can.

The younger Hazlitt—whether benefited by his father's advice or not—lived a long and fruitful life, dying at eighty-two after a career as a lawyer, translator and writer. His father, on the other hand, never learned to manage his personal life. "He has fallen in love, to a pitch of insanity," Benjamin Robert Haydon wrote, "with a lodging house hussy, who will be his death. He has been to Scotland and divorced his wife, although he has a fine little boy by her; and after doing this to marry this girl, he comes back and finds she has been making a fool of him in order to get presents, and in reality has been admitting a

lover more favoured. Hazlitt's torture is beyond expression . . ."
Perhaps as a purge, Hazlitt meticulously described his unhappy
love affair in *Libor Amoris or the New Pygmalion*. Shortly afterward he astonished his friends by marrying a widow, but this,
too, proved a disaster in little more than a year.

*   *   *

"Our real wants are but few . . ."

Andrew Jackson Hopes to Reform His Profligate Son:

The adopted son of General Jackson misinterpreted the fame
and fortune his father had struggled so hard to win. As early
as 1824 when Andrew, Jr., was a fourteen-year-old schoolboy,
it took him only six-and-a-half months to run up a bill of $309
at a general store. He was a spendthrift all his life. He also
drank too much, and indulged in love affairs. As a twenty-five-
year-old husband and father, he was $5,000 in debt when he
received this letter from his father in the White House.

April 14, 1835

. . .

    I now address you with the fondness of a father's heart.
How careful then ought you to be to shun all bad company, or
to engage in any dissipation whatever and particularly intoxica-
tion. When I reflect on the fate of your cousin Savern, reduced
to the contempt of all by his brutal intemperance I shudder when
I see any appearance of it in any branch of our connection . . .

[The happiness of] your charming little wife and sweet little ones depends on your upright course. This my son ought always to be before your eyes . . .

You must, *to get thro' life well,* practice industry and economy. . . . Nothing can be more disgraceful than the charge truly made that he has promised to pay money at a certain day, and violating that promise. Our real wants are but few, our imaginary wants many, which never ought to be gratified by creating a debt to supply them. These subjects [are] so essential to your happiness here and hereafter and that of your charming little family.

But young Andrew was immune to "industry and economy." When General Jackson died, he was $24,000 in debt on his son's account.

*   *   *

". . . your shrieks of anguish were so . . .
unexplained by . . . facts . . ."

William James Analyzes a Daughter's Emotional Problems:

Pioneer of the theory of pragmatism, William James had been beset as a youth by phobic troubles which were to lead him into his distinguished career as a psychologist. His physical health was never good, and in 1900 he and his wife were living at a German spa, and his thirteen-year-old daughter, Margaret, was in school in England. The child's effort to put her unhappiness on paper brought this response from her father:

Villa Luise
Bad Nauheim, May 26, 1900

Darling Peg,—Your letter came last night and explained sufficiently the cause of your long silence. You have evidently been in a bad state of spirits again, and dissatisfied with your environment; and I judge that you have been still more dissatisfied with the inner state of trying to consume your own smoke, and grin and bear it, so as to carry out your mother's behests made after the time when you scared us so by your inexplicable tragic outcries in those earlier letters. Well! I believe you have been trying to do the manly thing under difficult circumstances, but one learns only gradually to do the *best* thing; and the best thing for you would be to write at least weekly, if only a post-card, and say just how things are going. If you are in bad spirits, there is no harm whatever in communicating that fact, and defining the character of it, or describing it as exactly as you like. The bad thing is to pour out the *contents* of one's bad spirits on others and leave them with it, as it were, on their hands, as if it was for them to do something about it. That was what you did in your other letter which alarmed us so, for your shrieks of anguish were so excessive, and so unexplained by anything you told us in the way of facts, that we didn't know but what you had suddenly gone crazy. That is the *worst* sort of thing you can do. The middle sort of thing is what you do this time—namely, keep silent for more than a fortnight, and when you do write, still write rather mysteriously about your sorrows, not being quite open enough.

Now, my dear little girl, you have come to an age when the

inward life develops and when some people (and on the whole those who have most of a destiny) find that life is not a bed of roses. Among other things there will be waves of terrible sadness, which last sometimes for days; and dissatisfactions with one's self, and irritation at others, and anger at circumstances and stony insensibility, etc., etc., which taken together form melancholy. Now, painful as it is, this is sent to us for enlightenment. It always passes off, and we learn about life from it, and we ought to learn a great many good things if we react on it rightly. [From margin:] (For instance, you learn how good a thing your home is, and your country, and your brothers, and you learn to be more considerate of other people, who, you now learn, may have their inner weaknesses and sufferings, too.) Many persons take a kind of sickly delight in hugging it; and some sentimental ones may even be proud of it, showing a fine sorrowful kind of sensibility. Such persons make a regular habit of the luxury of woe. That is the worst possible reaction on it. It is usually a sort of disease, when we get it strong, arising from the organism having generated some poison in the blood; and we mustn't submit to it an hour longer than we can help, but jump at every chance to attend to anything cheerful or comic or take part in anything active that will divert us from our mean, pining inward state of feeling. When it passes off, as I said, we know more than we did before. And we must try to make it last as short a time as possible. The worst of it often is that, while we are in it, we don't *want* to get out of it. We hate it, and yet we prefer staying in it —that is a part of the disease. If we find ourselves like that, we must make ourselves do something different, go with people, speak cheerfully, set ourselves to some kind of hard work, make ourselves sweat, etc.; and that is the good way of reacting that makes of us a valuable character. The disease makes you think of *yourself* all the time; and the way out of it is to keep as busy as we can thinking of *things* and of *other people*—no matter what's the matter with our self.

I have no doubt that you are doing as well as you know how, darling little Peg; but we have to learn everything, and I also have no doubt that you'll manage better and better if you ever have any more of it, and soon it will fade away, simply leaving you with more experience. The great thing for you now, I should suppose, would be to enter as friendly as possible into the interests of the Clarke children. If you like them, or acted as if you liked them, you needn't trouble about the question of whether they like you or not. They probably will, fast enough; and if they don't, it will be their funeral, not yours. But this is a great lecture, so I will stop. The great thing about it is that it is all true . . .

Keep a merry heart—"time and the hour run through the roughest day"—and believe me ever your most loving

W. J.

*   *   *

Theodore Roosevelt Reviews His Son's Year
at School:

The spring and summer of 1901 gave Theodore Roosevelt the
most uncharacteristic months of his career. He had—as he put
it—"taken the veil" when he became Vice President in March.
Until McKinley was assassinated in September, the retired
Rough Rider attempted to relieve the doldrums of his un-
wanted job by studying law. In this period he wrote this
Rooseveltian advice to his oldest son.

Oyster Bay, May 7, 1901

Blessed Ted:

It was the greatest fun seeing you, and I really had a satis-
factory time with you, and came away feeling that you were doing well. I am entirely satisfied with your standing, both in your
studies and in athletics. I want you to do well in your sports, and
I want even more to have you do well in your books; but I do
not expect you to stand first in either, if so to stand could cause
you overwork and hurt your health. I always believe in going
hard at everything, but at the same time I want to keep the
sense of proportion. It is never worthwhile to absolutely ex-
haust one's self or to take big chances unless for an adequate
object. I want you to keep in training the faculties which would
make you, if the need arose, able to put your last ounce of pluck
and strength into a contest. But I do not want you to squander
these qualities. To have you play football as well as you do, and
make a good name in boxing and wrestling, and be cox of your
second crew, and stand second or third in your class in the studies,

26

is all right. I should be rather sorry to have you drop too near the middle of your class, because, as you cannot enter college until you are nineteen, and will therefore be a year later in entering life, I want you to be prepared in the best possible way, so as to make up for the delay. But I know that all you can do you will do to keep substantially the position in the class that you have so far kept, and I have entire trust in you, for you have always deserved it. . . .

* * *

*"As soon as a boy reaches
the age of discretion . . ."*

Gandhi Defines His Creed for Education in a Censored Letter:

An interviewer once asked, "May not an artist or a poet or a great genius leave a legacy of his genius to posterity through his children?" On November 20, 1924, in *Young India,* Gandhi replied: "Certainly not. He will have more disciples than he can ever have children." Gandhi has often been accused of making life more difficult for his sons than was necessary. "He expected Harilal, Manilal, Ramdas, Devadas to be chips off the old block, but the block did not chip," says Louis Fischer in his biography of the Mahatma. At the age of forty, Gandhi was serving his third prison term in Volksrust, South Africa, when he wrote to his second son, Manilal, aged seventeen. The letter was written with indelible purple ink on prison stationery which

27

bore the command to write in English, Dutch, German, French or Kafir. Thus prohibited from using his native Gujarati, Gandhi wrote in English as follows—the letter is dated March 25, 1909, Gandhi's number was 777, and the censor initialed it two days later.

My dear son, I have a right to write one letter per month and receive also one letter per month. It became a question with me as to whom I should write to. I thought of Mr. Rich [the editor of *Indian Opinion*], Mr. Polack and you. I chose you because you have been nearest my thoughts in all my reading.

. . . How are you? Although I think that you are well able to bear all the burden I have placed on your shoulders and that you are doing it quite cheerfully, I have often felt that you required greater personal guidance than I have been able to give you. I know too that you have sometimes felt that your education was being neglected. Now I have read a great deal in the prison. I have been reading Emerson, Ruskin and Mazzini. I have also been reading the *Upanishads*. All confirm the view that education does not mean a knowledge of letters but it means character building. It means a knowledge of duty. Our own [Gujarati] word literally means training. If this is the true view, and it is to my mind the only true view, you are receiving the best education-training possible. What can be better than that you should have the opportunity of nursing mother & cheerfully bearing her ill temper, or than looking after Chanchi & anticipating her wants and behaving to her so as not to make her feel the absence of Harilal or again than being guardian to Ramdas and Devadas? If you succeed in doing this well, you have received more than half your education.

I was much struck by one passage in Nathuramji's introduction to the *Upanishads*. He says that the Brahmacharya stage

—*i.e.*, the first stage, is like the last, *i.e.*, the sanyasin [monk] stage. This is true. Amusement only continues during the age of innocence, *i.e.*, up to twelve years only. As soon as a boy reaches the age of discretion, he is taught to realise his responsibilities. Every boy from such stage onward should practise continence in thought & deed, truth likewise and the not-taking of any life. This to him must not be an irksome learning and practise but it should be natural to him. It should be his enjoyment. I can recall to my mind several such boys in Rajkot. Let me tell you that when I was younger than you are my keenest enjoyment was to nurse my father. Of amusement after I was twelve, I had little or none. If you practise the three virtues, if they become part of your life, so far as I am concerned you will have completed your education—your training. Armed with them, believe me you will earn your bread in any part of the world & you will have paved the way to acquire a true knowledge of the soul, yourself and God. This does not mean that you shd not receive instruction in letters. That you shd & you are doing. But it is a thing over which you need not fret yourself. You have plenty of time for it and after all you are to receive such instruction in order that your training may be of use to others.

. . . Do give ample work to gardening, actual digging, hoeing, etc. We have to live upon it in the future. And you shd be the expert gardener of the family. Keep your tools in their respective places and absolutely clean. In your lessons you shd give a great deal of attention to mathematics and Sanskrit. The latter is absolutely necessary for you. Both these studies are difficult in after life. You will not neglect your music. You shd make a selection of all good passages, hymns and verses, whether in English, Gujarati or Hindi and write them out in your best hand in a book. The collection at the end of a year will be most valuable.

All these things you can do easily if you are methodical. Never get agitated and think you have too much to do and then worry over what to do first. This you will find out in practise if you are patient and take care of your minutes. I hope you are keeping an accurate account as it should be kept of every penny spent for the household.

. . . Please tell Maganlalbhai that I would advise him to read Emerson's essays. They can be had for nine pence in Durham. There is a cheap reprint out. These essays are worth studying. He shd read them, mark the important passages and then finally copy them out in a notebook. The essays to my mind contain the teaching of Indian wisdom in a western guru. It is interesting to see our own sometimes thus differently fashioned. He should also try to read Tolstoy's Kingdom of God is within you. It is a most logical book. The English of the translation is very simple. What is more Tolstoy practises what he preaches. . . .

And now I close with love to all and kisses to Ramdas, Devadas & Rami.

from
Father.

In 1916, Manilal, lent his brother, Harilal, who was struggling to become a businessman in Calcutta, some Gandhi funds that had been left in his charge. When the Mahatma discovered this, he ordered Manilal to apprentice himself to a hand spinner and to not use the Gandhi name. After this period of penance, Manilal was sent off to South Africa to edit *Indian Opinion,* and after that was permitted only occasional visits with his family. "The longest period I was able to spend in India, and most of it with father," Manilal told Louis Fischer, "was the whole of 1945 and half of 1946. Those were precious months . . . He was always forgiving, though he was a very severe taskmaster." Gandhi never used his influence to help his children. When Harilal's business ventures brought a protest from an investor "whose respect for Mahatmaji had led him to become a share-holder," Gandhi disavowed any responsibility. "Men may be good," he wrote, "not necessarily their children."

*   *   *

". . . the very wise, if any such there are . . ."

Jawaharlal Nehru Sends a Present from Prison to His Daughter:

There were some ironic differences between Gandhi and Nehru, though both spent much of their lives in jail. The seven terms Nehru served before he was fifty gave him considerable time for writing. Many of the letters he wrote from his cell were to his daughter—whom he encouraged in every way possible— who grew up to become his hostess when he was made prime minister, and whom he here addresses as "Priyadarshini," which means "Dear to the sight."

Central Prison, Naini
October 26, 1930
For Indira Priyadarshini on her thirteenth birthday.

On your birthday you have been in the habit of receiving presents and good wishes. Good wishes you will have in full measure, but what present can I send you from Naini Prison? My presents cannot be material or solid. They can only be of the air and of the mind and spirit, such as a good fairy might have bestowed on you—things that even the high walls of prison cannot stop.

You know, sweetheart, how I dislike sermonizing and doling out good advice . . . I am quite sure that there is no danger of my ever bursting with too much wisdom and so there is no need for me to wear copper plate or armor . . . If I am so limited in wisdom, how can I pose as a wise man and distribute good advice to others? And so I have always thought that the best way to find out what is right and what is not right, what should be done and what should not be done, is not by giving a sermon, but by talking and discussing, and out of discussion sometimes a little bit of truth comes out. I have liked my talks with you and we have discussed many things, but the world is wide and beyond our world lie many other wonderful and mysterious worlds so none of us need ever be bored or imagine, like the very foolish or conceited . . . that we have learned everything worth learning and become very wise. And perhaps it is as well we do not become very wise; for the very wise, if any such there are, must sometimes feel rather sad that there is nothing more to learn. They must miss the joy of discovery and learning new things—the great adventures that all of us who care to may have. . . .

Good-bye, little one, and may you grow up into a brave soldier in India's service.

With all my love and good wishes,

When she was twenty-four, Indira herself was sent to prison for following her father's political footsteps. She once said, "My public life started at the age of three. I have no recollection of playing games, or playing with other children. My favorite occupation as a small child was to deliver thunderous speeches to

32

the servants, standing on a high table." In 1959, still following the course set by her father, she was elected president of the Indian National Congress, the largest democratic body in the world.

✳   ✳   ✳

". . . consider your improving
in health paramount . . ."

Leopold Godowsky Reluctantly Leaves His Daughter in Europe:

In Hollywood's early days, one of its best-known vamps was a girl named Dagmar Godowsky. She was the daughter of the Austrian composer whom James G. Huneker called "the superman of the piano," and she said of herself that she had been "born on top of the world." Wherever her father stopped for breath, there quickly appeared a crowd of famous names. "Godowsky's home," wrote his friend Abram Chasins in *Speaking of Pianists,* "made Sanger's Circus seem like a rest home. Hubbub and commotion reigned day and night in four languages. Everyone and anyone was welcome. There seemed to be a perpetual party going on . . . His sons and daughters came naturally by their linguistic virtuosity and easy sociability." From this atmosphere, Dagmar Godowsky slipped easily into leading roles opposite Valentino and Lionel Barrymore, but neither a movie career nor two marriages minimized the warm rapport between father and daughter. And like many fathers who lead more ordinary lives, Leopold Godowsky could not forget the little girl in the woman of the world. In this letter he hoped to persuade Dagmar to give up some of the habits she had formed through her Hollywood exposures.

33

May 31st, 1933

My darling Dagmar:

It is now before breakfast. In several short hours we will be on the boat, sailing away from you, my dear child. I cannot tell you how painful and sad it is for me to part from you and leave you alone among strangers, but it is your wish, and you should stay away from us for awhile. You should not have *any* care but *your* health. Be careful, *very* careful with your diet; don't touch any wine, beer or other intoxicating drinks, and *learn* to sleep and rest much.

I would rather see you go to Danemark and *stay* there for the summer, than go on a taxing motor trip in warm countries. Your health would certainly be benefited by remaining in one cool bracing place and not sightseeing in hot cities.

So please, be sensible and prudent to consider your improving in health paramount to all else. Do it for yourself and for your parents, who love you dearly.

Should you get homesick or lonely, so that you would feel like joining us in America, cable me and I will secure your passage and send it (the ticket) without delay. . . . When you will be settled and have an address, let me know and I will send you money. You have been a very sweet, kind and good child, loving and lovable. You were lovely to your mother. God bless you!

With all my love and best wishes for your perfect health and happiness,

Your devoted
Pa

*   *   *

A Twentieth Century Writer's List of Do's and Don'ts:

F. Scott Fitzgerald was in the midst of work on *Tender Is the Night* when he wrote this characteristic letter to his eleven-year-old daughter in camp. Troubled by his wife's illness, and by the numerous crises in their marriage, he frequently found outlet in paternal letters. "You came along," he once wrote Scottie, "and for a long time we made quite a lot of happiness out of our lives." In the lines below, Fitzgerald shows a Twentieth Century approach to the kind of advice that concerned Jefferson in the letter on page 12.

> August 8, 1933
> La Paix, Rodgers' Forge
> Towson, Maryland

Dear Pie:

I feel very strongly about your doing duty. Would you give me a little more documentation about your reading in French? I am glad you are happy—but I never believe much in happiness. I never believe in misery either. Those are things you see on the stage or the screen or the printed page, they never really happen to you in life.

All I believe in in life is the rewards for virtue (according to your talents) and the *punishments* for not fulfilling your duties, which are doubly costly. If there is such a volume in the camp library, will you ask Mrs. Tyson to let you look up a sonnet of Shakespeare's in which the line occurs *Lilies that fester smell far worse than weeds.*

Have had no thoughts today, life seems composed of getting up a *Saturday Evening Post* story. I think of you, and always pleasantly; but if you call me "Pappy" again I am going to take the White Cat out and beat his bottom *hard, six times for every time you are impertinent.* Do you react to that?

I will arrange the camp bill.

Half-wit, I will conclude. Things to worry about:

> Worry about courage
> Worry about cleanliness
> Worry about efficiency
> Worry about horsemanship . . .

Things not to worry about:

> Don't worry about popular opinion
> Don't worry about dolls
> Don't worry about the past
> Don't worry about the future
> Don't worry about growing up
> Don't worry about anybody getting ahead of you
> Don't worry about triumph
> Don't worry about failure unless it comes through your own fault
> Don't worry about mosquitoes
> Don't worry about flies
> Don't worry about insects in general
> Don't worry about parents
> Don't worry about boys
> Don't worry about disappointments
> Don't worry about pleasures
> Don't worry about satisfactions

Things to think about:

> What am I really aiming at?

How good am I in comparison to my contemporaries
in regard to:
>   (a) Scholarship
>   (b) Do I really understand about people
>   and am I able to get along with them?
>   (c) Am I trying to make my body a useful
>   instrument or am I neglecting it?
>   With dearest love,

"Try something hard and new," Fitzgerald wrote Scottie seven
years later, "and try it hard, and take what marks you can get."

*   *   *

"I speak to you across the years
which lie between us . . ."

A Soldier of World War II Defines His Faith to an Unborn Child:

Robert A. Keyworth of Norwalk, Connecticut, joined the Army
in August, 1942, and became an Aviation Cadet. Eight months
later, while in training at Maxwell Field, Alabama, he wrote the
following message to his unborn child. "It best describes," said
Harry E. Maule in *The Book of War Letters*, "the heroic attitude
of the youth of the country who were brought up in an atmosphere
of cynicism and disillusionment."

37

Dear Son: I have no way of knowing as I write this, that you, my yet unborn child will be a boy. It is just that I find myself thinking of you as a boy and so, if you turn out to be a little lady, you must forgive your dad, for I will cherish you as I do your mother. I hope and pray that, at some future, happier time, when you are old enough to understand, I will be able to read you this myself. It may be, though, that you must read these lines alone and this is my reason in writing them.

The country that will in a few short weeks claim you as one of its newest citizens is fighting for its national existence. Your mother waits alone at home to bring you into the world while your father prepares for whatever may be his share of the combat which lies ahead. The risks are great and, though my comrades in uniform laugh with me as we joke of the future danger, still in each of our hearts is the quieting knowledge that some day soon we must prepare ourselves to face the final act of death.

That we can laugh now is a high tribute to the many reasons we have found to thus prepare ourselves and move forward in hope and courage.

Twenty-five years ago, when I was born, the world was also at war. I grew up during the peace that followed, totally unaware of the pain and sacrifice that had gone into the winning of that peace, however brief it may have been. I learned to sneer, with other schoolboys, at that merely preliminary battle "to make the world safe for Democracy." Not even knowing what Democracy meant, I repeated that phrase with words of scorn. War is for fools, I maintained. If they'd had any sense the whole thing could have been avoided. They *wanted* war!

In this matter, my son, my ignorance equalled my ego. This was the state of mind I found myself in when the men who now seek to destroy my country—and yours—plunged my world into the horror of total war. In what a short space of time did I discover what it meant to live in a free world!

I speak to you across the years which lie between us so that you will not be a partner to the derision and contempt in which many of your contemporaries will, inevitably, hold my generation. This fight we pursue is for you who will follow, for, in the winning of it, many of us will have lost all that gives to life its savour. We want only, at the close of it, to return to whatever is left of the world we knew and finish out our time in peace.

Even as I write these lines the dreams of many men are fading in their hearts, supplanted by the nightmare of war and all that war can mean to a man and a woman. These are the dreams we hold so dear, which we are so reluctant to let go, that are the very reason we seek to destroy our enemies at whatever cost. For these dreams of ours and of the men and women who came before us, built this country. They made your country, my son, the last asylum for the decent man who desires, not the sun but only a chance to work for a place in it. The men we fight would keep us chained in the shadow of their false greatness and so we oppose our strength to theirs. In this way we give to you who come after your chance to dream as we were offered our own.

Forgetting all else, son, remember what I say to you now. The Army in which I am a soldier provides a Corps of Chaplains to minister to the spiritual need of all men in uniform wherever on the globe they may find themselves. These men of God have given to me two words on which to base my courage and my hope of a better time. These simple words encompass all that I know, all that I would be able to tell you in ten thousand others. Accept them, use them each day that you live in all your dealings with people and situations and yours will be the happy life. They are: *Have faith.*

Away from your mother I am lonely and sad and the knowledge that I cannot be close to her when you draw your first breath gives me the greatest anguish I have ever known. My father and mother are old and frightened by the world's madness and are also alone. I know, that could I be with them, their pain would ease and their hearts lift. What, then, sustains me? Only my faith, for it has created between those I love and myself a tremendous bond, possessed of such strength that nothing can alter it. In this I find all my strength, all my courage, all my hope.

My faith allows me to look forward to the wonderful years that will come for us with victory and to the good things we will share together. God grant that this will be so. If it be otherwise then you must dream my dreams, fulfill your ambitions as I sought to fulfill my own, find the peace, the happiness, which I have only touched upon. Whatever happens, my son, may my blessing and that of God protect you and keep you.

Your Father

II

*   *   *

Family Circle

*. . . head of the household,
father of the bride . . . the male parent
shows his love, his anguish, and his dreams
as the family circle widens . . .*

". . . she retains in her company
our traitor and mortal foe . . ."

Edward II Asks His Young Son to Disown
His Mother's Infidelity:

Once described as "the first king after the Conquest who was not a man of business," Edward II permitted himself to be led by favorites whose wills were stronger than his own. Indeed, his wife —Isabella of France, sister of the new French monarch Charles the Fair—so scorned Edward that when he delegated his thirteen-year-old son to pay homage to Charles, she made it the opportunity to meet her paramour, Roger Mortimer, whom Edward had managed to have banished. After weeks of frustrating correspondence with both wife and son, the unhappy Edward could contain himself no longer. A father, he thought, was entitled to the loyalty of his scion, and he determined to bring the youngster home post haste. Edward's letters to his teen-age heir might well have been from man to man.

[1326]

Edward, My Fair Son,

We understand by your letters written in reply to ours that you remember well the charge we gave you; among other things, not to contract marriage, nor to suffer it to be contracted for you, without our knowledge or consent; and also that at your departure from Dover you said 'that it should be your pleasure to obey our commandments, as far as you could, all your days.'

Fair son, if thus you have done, you have done wisely and well, and according to your duty, so as to have grace of God and us and all men; and if not, then you cannot avoid the wrath of

43

God, the reproach of men, and our great indignation, for we charged you so lately and so strictly that you should remember well these things, and that you should by no means marry, nor suffer yourself to be married without our previous consent and advice; for no other thing that you could do would occasion greater injury and pain of heart to us. And inasmuch as it seems you say 'you cannot return to us because of your mother,' it causes us great uneasiness of heart that you cannot be allowed by her to do that which is your natural duty, and which not doing will lead to much mischief.

Fair son, you know how dearly she would have been loved and cherished, if she had timely come according to her duty to her lord. We have knowledge of much of her evil doings, to our sorrow; how that she devises pretences for absenting herself from us, on account of our dear and faithful nephew, H. le Despencer, who has always so well and loyally served us, while you and all the world have seen that she openly, notoriously, and knowing it to be contrary to her duty, and against the welfare of our crown, has attracted to herself, and retains in her company, the Mortimer, our traitor and mortal foe, proved, attainted, and adjudged, and *him* she accompanies in the house and abroad in despite of us, of our crown, and the right ordering of the realm—him, the malefactor whom our beloved brother the king of France at our request banished from his dominions as our enemy! And worse than this she has done, *if* worse than *this* can be, in allowing you to consort with our said enemy, making him your counsellor, and you openly to herd and associate with him in the sight of all the world, doing so great a villainy and dishonor both to yourself and us to the prejudice of our crown, and of the laws and customs of our realm,

44

which *you* are supremely bound to hold, preserve, and maintain.

Wherefore, fair son, desist you from a part which is so shameful, and may be to you perilous and injurious in too many ways. We are not pleased with you, and neither for your mother, nor for any other, ought you to displease us. We charge you by the faith, love, and allegiance which you owe us, and on our blessing, that you come to us without opposition, delay, or any further excuse; for your mother has written to us, 'that if you wish to return to us she will not prevent it,' and we do not understand that your uncle the king detains you against the form of your safe conduct. In no manner, then, either for your mother, or to go to the duchy, nor for any other cause, delay to come to us. Our commands are for your good, and for your honour, by the help of God. Come quickly, then, without further excuse, if you would have our blessing, and avoid our reproach and indignation.

It is our wish to order all things for the good of the duchy, and our other dominions, for our mutual honour and benefit.

If John of Bretagne, and John of Cromwell, will come in your company, they will do their duty.

Fair son, trespass not against our commands, for we hear too much that you have done of things you ought not.

Given at Lichfield, the 18th day of March.

Not until September did the boy prince return—accompanied by his mother and Mortimer. The queen declared that she had come to expel Hugh le Despenser, and rallied the barons and the populace to her cause. With Mortimer commanding her troops, she chased King Edward and his adherents to the Irish Sea, killing Despenser and his son, and capturing her husband. Edward was deposed and his heir elected in his place. It was only after three years had passed, when young Edward III arrested Mortimer in his mother's room, that one of his father's hopes was fulfilled. Mortimer was summarily executed.

*　　　*　　　*

*"You will think I need not advise you
to love your Wife!"*

Oliver Cromwell Offers His Successor Some Rambling Advice:

Four years away from the Lord Protectorship, Oliver Cromwell was nearing the end of his victorious campaign in Ireland when he took time out from battle to write the peaceful letter below. His twenty-four-year-old son, taking no part in Cromwell's battles, had recently been married and was living the life of a country gentleman in Hampshire.

Carrick, 2d April 1650

Dick Cromwell,—I take your Letters kindly: I like expression when they come plainly from the heart, and are not strained nor affected.

I am persuaded it's the Lord's mercy to place you where you are: I wish you may own it and be thankful, fulfilling all relations to the glory of God. Seek the Lord and His face continually;—let this be the business of your life and strength, and let all things be subservient and in order to this! You cannot find nor behold the face of God but Christ; therefore labour to know the God in Christ: which the Scripture makes to be the sum of

46

all, ever transforming the mind to it. It's writing to, and participating of the Divine Nature (Second Peter, i. 4): "Whereby are given unto us exceeding great and precious promises: that by these ye might be partakers of the divine nature, having escaped the corruption that is in the world through lust." It's such a knowledge as Paul speaks of (Philippians, iii, 8-10): "Yea doubtless, and I count all things but loss for the excellency of the knowledge of Christ Jesus my Lord: for whom I have suffered the loss of all things, and do count them but dung, that I may win Christ, And be found in Him, not having mine own righteousness, which is of the law, but that which is through the faith of Christ, the righteousness which is of God by faith: That I may know him, and the power of his resurrection, and the fellowship of his sufferings, being made comformable unto his death;" . . . How little of this knowledge is among us! My weak prayers shall be for you.

Take heed of an unactive vain spirit! Recreate yourself with Sir Walter Raleigh's History: it's a Body of History; and will add much more to your understanding than fragments of Story. —Intend to understand the Estate I have settled: it's your concern to know it all, and how it stands. I have heretofore suffered much by too much trusting others. I know my brother Mayor [the younger Cromwell's father-in-law] will be helpful in all this.

You will think, perhaps, I need not advise you to love your Wife! The Lord teach you how to do it;—or else it will be done ill-favouredly. Though Marriage be no instituted Sacrament, yet where the undefiled bed is, and love, this union aptly resembles "that of" Christ and His Church. If *you* can truly love your Wife, what "love" doth Christ bear to His Church and every poor soul therein,—who "gave Himself" for it and to it!

—Commend me to your Wife; tell her I entirely love her, and rejoice in the goodness of the Lord to her. I wish her every way fruitful. I thank her for her loving Letter . . .

—Dick, the Lord bless you in every way. I rest, your loving Father,

Oliver Cromwell

Marriage was indeed sacred to the elder Cromwell. He had been a husband for thirty years when he wrote to the mother of his eight children, "Thou art dearer to me than any creature; let that suffice." Richard Cromwell never became the man his father was. Though appointed Lord Protector at his father's behest, he had no gift for even inherited leadership. He was soon deposed, and he fled to the Continent where he lived under an assumed name for twenty years. He was once described as "gentle and virtuous but a peasant in his nature and became not greatness."

*   *   *

". . . a good wife . . . yet . . . I must believe you will be as good a daughter . . ."

James II Beseeches the Loyalty of the Princess of Orange:

When Charles II reigned in England, he approved the marriage of his niece Mary to his nephew William of Orange, and thereby set the stage for heartbreak. Mary's father, who became James II, was a militant Catholic, but his two daughters had been reared in the Anglican church. Thus it was on Mary, and on her sister, the Princess of Denmark, that Protestant England staked its hopes—for in the fifteen years of James's second marriage he had had no other children. Then, in 1688, a son was born, and the king's enemies knew that they must strike immediately or not at all. A delegation was sent to persuade William of Orange to depose James, thus putting the king in the position of having to fight his eldest daughter as well as his son-in-law. Mary, siding with her husband and the Protestants, sought to divert her father from taking seriously the rumors of William's invasion plans, corresponding with him until a few days before the landings.

Whitehall, Oct. 9, 1688

I had no letter from you by the last post, which you see does not hinder me from writing to you now, not knowing, certainly, what may have hindered you from doing it. I easily believe you may be embarrassed how to write to me now, that the unjust design of the prince of Orange's invading me is so public.

And though I know you are a good wife, and ought to be so, yet for the same reason, I must believe you will be still as good a daughter to a father that has always loved you so tenderly, and that has never done the least thing to make you doubt it. I shall say no more, and believe you very uneasy all this time, for the concern you must have for a husband and a father. You shall still find me kind to you if you desire it.

While James was thus writing to Mary, his brother-in-law tried equally to arouse some filial devotion in James's younger daughter Anne, Princess of Denmark. No persuasion availed, and William of Orange embarked on the first favorable wind. On October tenth, the king and his brother-in-law met again. "I have nothing by this day's post from my daughter, the Princess of Orange," he said, "and it is the first time I have missed hearing from her for a long time." He never heard from Mary again. Soon he found that Anne and her Danish husband had gone over to William,

and he cried out, "God help me! My children have forsaken me!"
On December twenty-second, James stole out of England forever,
and shortly thereafter Mary—with William of Orange reigning
jointly—succeeded her father.

Six years later, at the age of thirty-three, the most virulent
form of smallpox took Queen Mary's life. Her father's adherents
were quick to speak their minds. Among the epigrams preserved
in manuscript is this Jacobite epitaph:

> Here ends, notwithstanding her specious pretences,
> The undutiful child of the kindest of princes;
> Well, here let her lie, for by this time she knows,
> What it is such a father and king to dispose;
> Between vice and virtue, she parted her life,
> She was too bad a daughter, and too good a wife.

✳   ✳   ✳

> *". . . the aid and comfort an affectionate*
> *son can give . . ."*

Boswell Is Summoned Home from Europe on His Mother's Death:

Though James Boswell loved his mother dearly, he very seldom
wrote to her or she to him; the letters from home were written
by the young man's father, Lord Auchinleck. In 1765, at twenty-
five years of age, Boswell was traveling in Europe. He spent
eleven months in Italy, with an excursion which produced his
famous *Account of Corsica,* and in December of that year he was
in Paris, slowly working his way toward his home in Scotland.

His leisurely plans changed when he received news of his mother's death.

Edinburgh, 30 January 1766

Upon the 11 of this month I wrote you the account of the death of your excellent mother, who was no *bel esprit*, no wit, no genius, but one who endeavoured to make her husband, children, friends, and all around her happy; who lived the life of a true practical Christian, exerting herself with diligence in doing her duty without intermission to God and her fellow creatures, and whose end was peace. Her exit, which she made with the greatest satisfaction, as my former particularly mentioned, has left me in a most desolate state; and as I therein desired you might come home speedily, as I needed all the aid and comfort an affectionate son can give, I have been counting with impatience when I may expect to see you here and flatter myself that it will be in a few days. For although I had a letter from Dr. Pringle acquainting me of some proposals you had bid him mention to me from Lyons, and a letter from yourself from Paris containing another very strange proposal, I have reason, I think, to hope that the melancholy news I wrote you would immediately put an end to that fermentation, and make you think seriously what you owe to duty, to gratitude, and to interest.

If that be so, all is well. But if contrary to expectation you shall be unmoved, and go on in pursuit of a scheme which you in your unstayed state are absolutely unfit for at present, and a scheme, which, abstracting from that, is improper and would be ruinous—a foreigner, a *bel esprit* and one who even in your own opinion has not solidity enough for this country—what can you expect from me? All that I need say further is that as I gave you a full allowance to answer your expenses in every place you

5 1

were in and you have got all that advanced and considerably more; and as I ordered you one hundred pounds at Paris, which was to defray your expense the few days you stayed there and bring you over to London; if you shall employ that money for other purposes, it is what I cannot prevent, but I acquaint you that I am to answer no more of your bills, either for one purpose or another. I hope there will be no occasion for this last *caveat*, as I hope you will show yourself a dutiful and affectionate son, as I have been, and wish to continue, your affectionate father,

Alexr. Boswel. [The father's spelling.]

Boswell didn't arrive home until two months later. He wrote on the margin of the above: "This letter arrived at Paris after I had left it, and lay at Foley's [Boswell's banker] until July, 1766, when I got it over to Scotland."

✻   ✻   ✻

> *". . . the little remainder of life with my family . . ."*

Benjamin Franklin Discusses the Pros and Cons of Dying Abroad:

Franklin was seventy when he arrived in France as Ambassador from the United States. He spent more than eight years in Paris, and made so many friends that there were temptations, considering his health, to await his fate far from his native soil. But his

5 2

daughter and his grandchildren—and his feeling of identity with the new nation he had helped to make—pushed him toward an expedition that promised little reward. Only a man who knew that his daughter and son-in-law (Sarah and Richard Bache) understood him could have written:

Passy, May 10, 1785

Dear Son and Daughter: Having at length received from Congress permission to return home, I am now preparing for my departure, and hope to get away by the middle of next month, or the end at farthest, though I know not yet whether it will be by the packet or some other vessel. Fearing that the packet may be crowded with passengers, I have desired my cousin, Jonathan Williams, now in London, to inquire whether there may not be found some good vessel bound directly to Philadelphia, who would agree to take me on board at Havre, with my grandsons and servants, with my baggage, etc. Infirm as I am, I have need of comfortable room and accommodation. I was miserably lodged in coming over hither, which almost demolished me. I must be better stowed now, or I shall not be able to hold out the voyage. Indeed my friends here are so apprehensive for me that they press me much to remain in France, and three of them have offered me an asylum in their habitations. They tell me I am here among a people who universally esteem and love me; that my friends at home are diminished by death in my absence; that I may there meet with envy and its consequent enmity which here I am perfectly free from: this supposing I live to complete the voyage, but of that they doubt. The desire, however, of spending the little remainder of life with my family is so strong as to determine me to try at least whether I can bear the motion of the ship. If not, I must get them to set me on shore somewhere in the Channel, and content myself to die in Europe.

It is long since I have heard from you or of you. I hope, however, that you and the children continue well. Ben is very well, and grows amazingly. He promises to be a stout as well as good man. Temple has been ill lately with a fever, but is getting better and sends his duty. I suppose Ben writes. I am ever, my dear children, your affectionate father.

Franklin made the journey without mishap. In 1787, when he was eighty, he was appointed a delegate to the Constitutional Convention, in which he played an important part. His will to be busy continued with almost no abatement. He built three houses; he wrote scientific papers; he argued, in print, for the abolition of slavery. Finally his time came. Among his daughter, his son-in-law and his grandchildren he died—on April 17, 1790. Philadelphia gave him a magnificent funeral, and the French Assembly went into mourning for three days.

*　　*　　*

". . . the lady whom I regarded as my wife . . ."

Dumas *Père* Accuses His Son of Disregarding His Mistress:

Though born out of wedlock, Alexandre Dumas *fils* was formally recognized by his father; indeed the elder Dumas applied for legal custody. But the boy was not to grow up with either of his parents. At the age of seven he was taken in charge by the police commissioner and sent to a boarding school. His sympathy for his mother remained uppermost all his life, and not until he was an adult did he come to understand his father. He once said, "My father is a great big child whom I had as a little boy." At the age of sixteen, Dumas *fils* saw the publication of the banns preceding his father's marriage to Ida Ferrier, a long-time mistress, and he wrote a letter expressing his opposition. Dumas *père's* reaction is astonishing.

[January 1840]

It is not my fault, but yours, that the relationship between us is no longer that of father and son. You came to my house, where you were well received by everyone, and then, suddenly, acting upon whose advice I do not know, decided no longer to recognize the lady whom I regarded as my wife, as should have been obvious from the fact that I was living with her. From that day, since I had no intention of taking advice (even indirectly) from you, the situation of which you complain, began and has lasted, much to my sorrow, for six years.

It can cease whenever you wish. You have only to write a letter to Madame Ida, asking her to be to you what she is to your sister; you will then be always, and eternally, welcome. The happiest thing that could happen to you is that this liaison should continue, since, having had no child for six years, I am now certain that I never shall have any, so that you are now not only my eldest, but my only, son.

I have nothing else to tell you. All that I would have you consider is this, that, should I marry any woman other than Madame Ida, I might well have three or four more children, whereas with her, I shall have none.

I trust that in all this you will consult your heart rather than your interests, though this time—contrary to what usually happens—the two are in agreement. I embrace you with all my heart.

After completing his education, the younger Alexandre did try to live with his father and stepmother, but not for long. When finally, at twenty, he insisted upon leaving, his father protested:

"You know that Madame Dumas is Madame Dumas only in name, whereas you are truly my son, and not only my son, but well-nigh the only happiness and distraction that I have . . . It must be quite obvious that I belong wholly to you, whereas you only half belong to me . . ."

*　　*　　*

*". . . I shall have the strength
to acknowledge everything . . ."*

Dumas Dismisses the Criticism of His Daughter:

There was an ironic difference in Dumas *père's* relationship with his natural daughter, Marie-Alexandrine, the sister referred to in the letter on page 55. He refused to let Marie's actress mother see the child, and she was brought up by "Madame Ida," whom she loved devotedly. When Ida left Dumas to live in Italy, Marie asked Ida "on bended knee to let me come back to you"—because she did not want to live among her father's mistresses. She did, however, stay with Dumas, and he enlisted her help in his multiple love affairs—a chore that offered her the malicious delight of provoking warfare among his women. When Marie was twenty-one and learned that a young housewife was with child by him, she sternly admonished her parent. His answer follows.

[Sometime in the winter of 1850–51]

Dear Marie, I have one or two serious things to say in reply to your letter. I don't see the matter in the same light as you. You consider it from the sentimental point of view: I propose to examine it from the social, and especially, from the human one.

Each of us is responsible for his faults, and even for his infirmities. No one has the right to lay the weight of them upon the shoulders of others. If an accident, or some physical malformation has resulted in this, that or the other man being impotent, it is for him to bear the consequences of that infirmity, and face them fairly and squarely, whatever form they may take.

If a woman has been guilty of a fault; if she has allowed herself to forget what she looked upon as a duty, then it is for her to atone for her weakness with strength, as a crime may be atoned for with repentance. But no woman who has been guilty of a fault, no man afflicted with impotence, has the right to shift onto the back of a third person the burden of her personal fault, or the consequences of his misfortune.

Before ever the child was conceived, I had been aware of these objections. They were carefully weighed, and my conclusions may be stated thus: *for the sake of the child I shall have the strength to acknowledge everything, and to see that everything turns out for the best.* It was the result of this determination of mine that the being who does not yet exist, who has been condemned in advance, was set in train.

Nothing would have been easier than *not* to have forced birth on a being who, now that he is on the way, though not yet born, is already in the position of being refused social recognition. Children of adultery can be acknowledged neither by the father or the mother. This one, therefore, will be doubly branded by the fact of adultery.

What will be his position with a mother in the state of health we all know—her opinion is that she may die at any moment—and a father already old who, by asking for another fifteen years of life, might seem to be making an excessive request? By the time it is fourteen, the child may find itself stranded without resources in a hostile world.

If it turns out to be a girl, and a pretty one, she will at least be able to register with the police and go on the streets at ten francs a time. If it is a boy, he will play the part of an Antony until such a time as he may, perhaps, play that of a Lacenaire.[1]

In that case it would be better to destroy a life, and better still not to create it. But it would anger me should such a decision be taken as the result of sentimental mawkishness. It would do violence to all my ideas on the subject of justice and injustice. It would deprive you of some part of my esteem, and, with that part of my esteem, I very much fear, of all my love.

Monsieur is impotent—and so much the worse for him. Madame has been weak—so much the worse for her. But let no one dare say 'so much the worse for the being that owes its life to that impotence and that weakness.' Each of us risked something in the action in which both of us were involved. Madame X . . . risked an action for divorce, and so determined was she to face the possibility that it was arranged that she should send me a copy of her marriage contract—which, in point of fact, she has not done. I, for my part, risked a sword-thrust or a pistol-shot, and that is a risk I am still perfectly prepared to run.

The child born as the result of Dumas's "risks" was later described as "the living image" of his father, but the name he bore, Henry Bauër, was that of his mother's husband. This son had considerable company according to Dumas *père* who estimated, toward the end of his life, that he had five hundred children in various parts of the world.

✳   ✳   ✳

[1] Antony, a character in one of Dumas's plays, was a social rebel and a bastard unable to marry the girl he loved. Lacenaire was a murderer, a self-styled enemy of society executed in 1836.

"... nor can ... tumbling waters hide
my group of loves ..."

Bronson Alcott Describes the Originals
of *Little Women:*

Late in life, after the troublous years caused by her father's inability to provide for his family, Louisa May Alcott defined a philosopher as "a man up in a balloon, with his family and friends holding the ropes which confine him to earth and trying to haul him down." Yet few fathers ever had more adoration than Louisa and her sisters gave their philosopher parent—or more constant admiration than Alcott drew from his friend Ralph Waldo Emerson. The Sage of Concord raised money to send Bronson to England when a school, based on Alcott's advanced theories, was established there. Basking, for a moment at least, in the friendlier climate he found abroad, Bronson wrote nostalgically to the girls who had stayed with their mother in Massachusetts.

For Louisa May Alcott,
Elizabeth Sewell Alcott
      and
Abba May Alcott

           Concordia Cottage—from their father,
           15 July, 1842

My dear Girls:

    I think of you all every day and desire to see you all again: Abba with her beauty-loving eyes and sweet visions of graceful motions, of golden hues and all fair and mystic shows and shapes —Louisa with her quick and ready services, her agile limbs and boundless curiosity, her penetrating mind and tear-shedding heart, alive to all moving, breathing things—Elizabeth with her quiet-loving disposition and serene thoughts, her happy gentleness, deep sentiment, self-centered in the depths of her affections —and last, but yet dearest too in her joys and impetuous griefs, the little Abba with her fast falling footsteps, her sagacious eye and auburn locks . . . and mother too, whose unsleeping love and painstaking hands provide for your comforts and pleasant things and is your hope and stay and now more near and important to you while I am taken from your eyes. All and each of you I have in my mind: daily I see you in my thoughts and as I lay my head on my pillow at night or wake from sleep in the morning . . . nor can the tumbling waters hide my group of loves from my eyes: the little cottage there behind the Elm, the garden round, strawberry red or colored vines . . . or corn barn play house, or street or bridge or winding stream, or Anna or Louisa, their lessons loved (and learned by heart, not rote) and Lizzie too with little Ab in parlor, study, chamber, lawn, with needle, book or pen . . . and so you see, my gentle girls, I cannot leave you quite: though my body is far away my mind is near and all the while, I hear and see and touch and think and feel your very selves—the life that lives in all you are and say and do, the mind, the Heart, the Soul—the God that dwells in you. And now be loving little girls and grow far more fair with every day and when I come to see my garden plot then shall my flowers scent the fields and I shall joy in every scent they lend, in every tint and form they wear. So now, my dears, adieu.

Let mother read this with you and talk long and sweetly with her about what is in it and then kiss her all and each other and then her all again for Father's sake.

Alcott admitted to his diary that "I must stand, for the time, as a thriftless, if not a heartless and insufferable fellow," but he never managed to lift the burden he placed on his daughters and their mother. They remained faithful to the end. Louisa May Alcott, writing frantically at times to support her father's family, never married. Two days after his death at eighty-nine, she died—

perhaps from the shock of realizing she no longer had him to care for.

* * *

". . . a great misfortune to outlive
my children . . ."

Daniel Webster Announces the Death of a Son in War:

Eloquent though he was in his orations, Daniel Webster was the most restrained of men in revealing his innermost self. Grief made him seem cold and unfeeling. Either he said as little as possible, or he took refuge in mawkish doggerel. His second surviving son, Edward, was a major who died of typhoid fever during the Mexican War. Webster was in his Senate office when he received the notice from the War Department, and he wrote immediately to Fletcher Webster.

February 23, 2 o'clock, 1848.
My Dear and Only Son: I have just received this; when shown to Julia and the rest of the family, send it back safely to me.

My own health is pretty good, but I hardly know how I shall bear up under this blow. I have always regarded it as a great misfortune to outlive my children; but I feel now, more intensely, as when Grace and Charles died.

But the will of Heaven be done in all things!

Yours affectionately,
Daniel Webster

Two months later, Webster's daughter Julia died, and the soldier and his sister were buried the same week. To mark their memory, Webster himself planted two elm trees in front of his Massachusetts home, then turned to Fletcher and said, "My son, protect these trees after I am gone. Let them ever remind you of Julia and Edward." What he felt about the loss of his children he once tried to put into verse:

> My son, thou wast my heart's delight;
> Thy morn of life was gay and cheery;
> That morn was rushed to sudden night,
> Thy father's house is sad and dreary.
> I held thee on my knee, my son!
> And kissed thee laughing, kissed thee weeping;
> But ah! thy little day is done,
> Thou'rt with thy angel sister sleeping.

* * *

"Hold fast this mystic power . . ."

Prince Albert Tells Princess Victoria What Her Marriage Means—to Him and to Her:

The first-born child of Albert and Victoria married Prince Frederick William of Prussia when she was seventeen, and the following year she gave birth to a son who became the Kaiser of World War I. So close were Princess Victoria and her father that historians believe Albert's influence, had he lived, might have been felt by his grandson. But in 1861, less than four years after his daughter's wedding, Albert was dead. The first of the letters below was written after the young couple returned from a brief honeymoon, the second after Princess Victoria had left her family for good.

Buckingham Palace

3rd Feb. 1858

My heart was very full when yesterday in the saloon you laid your head on my breast to give free vent to your tears. I am not of a demonstrative nature, and therefore you can hardly know how dear you have always been to me, and what a void you have left behind in my heart; yet not in my heart, for there assuredly you will abide henceforth, as till now you have done, but in daily life, which is evermore reminding my heart of your absence.

After Princess Victoria left England to live in Germany with Frederick William, her father wrote again:

Buckingham Palace

11th Feb. 1858

You have now entered upon your new home, and been received and welcomed on all sides with the greatest friendship and cordiality. This kindly and trustful advance of a whole nation towards an entire stranger must have kindled and confirmed within you the determination to show yourself in every way worthy of such feelings, and to reciprocate and requite them by the steadfast resolution to dedicate the whole energies of your life to this people of your new home. And you have received from Heaven the happy task of effecting this object by making your husband truly happy, and of doing him at the same time the best service, by aiding him to maintain and to increase the love of his countrymen.

That you have everywhere made so favourable an impression has given intense happiness to me as a father. Let me express my fullest admiration of the way which, possessed exclusively by the duty which you had to fulfil, you have kept down and overcome your own personal troubles, perhaps also many feelings of sorrow not yet healed. This is the way to success, and the *only* way. If you have succeeded in winning people's hearts by friendliness, simplicity, and courtesy, the secret lay in this, that you were not thinking of yourself. Hold fast this mystic power, it is a spark from Heaven.

To Him who shaped everything so happily, I am grateful from the very depths of my soul for the happy climax to the most important period of your life. Dear Child, I would have fain been in the crowd to see your entrance, and to hear what the multitude said of you; so, too, it is with Mama. We are, however, kept admirably informed of everything by the telegraph, and post, and papers. The telegraph must have been amazed when it wrote: "The whole Royal Family is enchanted with my wife.—F. W."

Our old marriage day [Albert and Victoria were married February 10, 1840] passed off yesterday quietly, but too much interrupted and overlaid with business of all sorts for calm enjoyment.

Albert filled his letters to the princess with counsel on her flair for art, on German politics, on happiness. Once he wrote that he yielded to "the feeling, sweetest of all to my heart as your father, that you will be lastingly happy." When she came to visit, he urged her to read Tennyson to him, and when he died she was painting scenes from *Idylls of the King* at his suggestion.

*   *   *

"Fair fall the little boy—
he has come among good people."

Emerson Congratulates His Daughter on the Birth of His Grandson:

It has been said that Emerson, "for an abstract thinker, was strangely in love with the concrete facts of life." He was a devoted husband and a wise and tender father, who wrote many letters to his children whenever he was off on his frequent speaking trips. He was at home in the "old house" in Concord when news of the birth of his first grandchild arrived and he sat down to put on paper the thoughts that event inspired.

> Concord
> 11 Evening
> [July 11, 1866]

My dear Edith,

Happy wife & Mother that you are—& not the less surely that the birth of your babe touches this old house & its people & neighbors with unusual joy. I hope the best gifts & graces of his father & mother will combine for this blossom, & highest influences hallow & ripen the firm & perfect fruit. There is nothing in this world so serious as the advent of a child with all his possibilities to parents with good minds & hearts. Fair fall the little boy—he has come among good people. I do not grudge to William & you the overflow of fondness & wonder,—& to the boy it is the soft pillow prepared for him—and (?) it is long before he will come to himself,—but I please myself already that his fortunes will be worthy of these great days of his country, that he will not be frivolous, that he will be noble & true, & will know what is sacred. I send affectionate congratula-

tions to William with our joint thanks here for his carefull &
successful forwarding of the tidings, & to Mrs Forbes for every
syllable of her welcome letter.

Your Mother joins me in this writing & sending, & adds
after her way but quite sincerely, a text for your reading, which
I too find in my bible, Luke, Chapter 1. verse 63.

Your loving father,
R. W. Emerson

*   *   *

"She sends him the Bill of her Milliner."

George Meredith Thinks His Daughter
Too Involved in Courting:

The author of *The Ordeal of Richard Feverel* and *Diana of the
Crossways* was left a widower with a son and daughter. After
his wife's death in 1885, the young Marie, or Mariette, Meredith
was the great joy of her father, who called her "Riette" or "My
Own Dearie." When she married and had daughters of her own,
Meredith was as delightedly involved with his grandchildren
as he had been with their mother. He was a great hand at dashing
off verse instead of a letter, but in either prose or poetry his pen
flowed with the intimacy he felt for his family.

Box Hill, July 10, 1891

To Miss Marie Meredith.

She scarce has a word for her Papa.
To tell how she carolled and sported O!

66

So, with just, How d'ye do and Ta-ta,
    She runs from her pen to be courted O!

To write were a foolish endeavour,
    But, to show that her humour is still in her,
And flourishing fatter than ever,
    She sends him the
        Bill of her Milliner.

*   *   *

"I have been and still am
full of weaknesses . . ."

Tolstoy Turns a Daughter's Mind to Some Marital Problems:

Certainly the lack of success of his own marriage sharpened the sense of loss felt by Leo Tolstoy when his daughter, Masha, announced her wish to marry her distant cousin, the penniless and spoiled Prince Nikolai Obolenski. She had been her father's constant companion. According to Alexandra Tolstoy, it was "Masha who glided noiselessly into his study with her father's freshly copied manuscript, who caught every fleeting thought, who lived his life, his interest; Masha who sensed so fully the joy of service; Masha, the sensitive, the spiritually-minded." Though Masha's choice made him uneasy, Tolstoy did not attempt to dissuade her. To crystallize his thoughts after her announcement, he sat in his study and wrote his daughter as follows:

Masha, there is nothing I have to say against your intentions, called forth, as I can see, by your yearning for marriage . . . Judging by your life recently, which has been more luxurious than formerly, and judging by the life and habits of Kolya . . . you are going to need a lot of money . . . This is very difficult and indeed too obvious—the exchange of independence, tranquility, for the most complex and painful sufferings. How do you weigh this? What does he think about it? . . . Do you intend to ask that your inheritance be given you? Does he intend to take a job and, if so, where? And please put aside any thought . . . that your rescinding of your intention to not accept your inheritance could change my esteem of you. I know and love you beyond and deeper than that, and none of your weaknesses can change my understanding of you and my love for you bound up with it. I have been and still am full of weaknesses and therefore I know how sometimes and indeed often they gain the upper hand. But there is just one thing: I may lie under my enemy's weight, I am in his power, yet I still cry out that I will not surrender, and once I can deal with him again I shall battle him. I know that you too will act in the same way, so do it. Only one must think, one must think very hard."

What thinking Masha did failed to deter her, for she was genuinely in love. She retrieved her inheritance and she and "Kolya" lived happily until her death in her thirty-fifth year. While she lived, Masha continued to be closest to Tolstoy of all his family. "I am indeed given to loving you and being loved by you," he wrote three months after the wedding. "Do I feel the break since your marriage? Yes, I feel it but I do not wish to feel it and I will not. . . ."

John Burroughs Entreats His Son to Marry Before He Is Twenty-four:

The great naturalist, John Burroughs, once wrote that he longed to go to college with his son "and be his chum." As a matter of fact, albeit vicariously, he lived his offspring's life as intimately as any father ever did. When Julian Burroughs was at Harvard, the naturalist shared all the young man's problems—his studies, his outside reading, his plans for a career, his deportment. It was as if John Burroughs, in his sixties, was at last given the chance to go to college himself. The maturing of his son supplied a need not filled by his marriage, for though Burroughs may have been fond of his wife, he could not share her materialistic views. She was devoted to him and their son, but she was not interested in his philosophic and scientific speculations, and was no intellectual company for him. Within the family circle he found his only real companionship with his son.

[1898]

. . . Your views of life, and of the things worth having, agree with my own . . . It is becoming very plain to me that you are cut out for a man of letters. This is as I would have it. Throw your whole soul into it, and do not mind the discouragements of your Mother. Her ideals, you know, do not go beyond wealth and respectability.

I shall be greatly disappointed, though, if you do not, in due time, make up your mind to marry. It is the proper thing to do, and is the way to rivet yourself to the world and to life. It is the order of nature. Love some sweet, gentle girl and make her your wife before you are twenty-four. It will make you a broader, more tender, more effective man and writer.

The farm, with my income from the books, and my pen will keep us all nicely till you can earn money yourself. You must have a career of your own, and I know you have enough push and ambition to carve out one.

I think you better drop Howells for a time. You do not want to get under his dominion. He is not a big enough man. Read Tolstoy, Hawthorne, Thackeray, and the French novelists, and then aim to see things for yourself, as they do . . .

With much love and deep solicitude for your well-being

Your affectionate father

J. B.

*   *   *

"I have already poured my heart out . . ."

Mark Twain Writes in Anguish After a Daughter's Death:

Widowed and in the last year of his life, Mark Twain was living at his country house, Stormfield, in Redding, Connecticut, with his daughter Jean when the latter became suddenly ill and died. The only surviving child was Clara, who had recently been married to Ossip Gabrilowitsch and was in Europe on a wedding trip.

Redding, Conn. Dec. 29, '09

O, Clara, Clara dear, I am so glad she is out of it and safe —safe! I am not melancholy; I shall never be melancholy again, I think. You see, I was in such distress when I came to realize you were gone far away and no one stood between her and danger but me—and I could die at any moment, and *then*,—oh then what would have become of her! For she was wilful, you know, and would not have been governable.

You can't imagine what a darling she was, that last two or three days: and how *fine*, and good, and sweet, and noble—and *joyful*, thank Heaven!—and how intellectually brilliant. I had never been acquainted with Jean before. I recognized that.

But I mustn't write about her—I *can't*. I have already poured my heart out with pen, recording that last day or two. I will send you that—and you must let no one but Ossip read it.

Good-bye. I love you so!! And Ossip.

Father

Poured from Mark Twain's heart was the essay "The Death of Jean" which was not published until after his own death.

✼　　✼　　✼

"I could tell 'em a thing or two
if I had a whack at 'em."

Ambassador Walter Hines Page Tells His Daughter What He Feels About Her Marriage:

During World War I, Theodore Roosevelt wrote that publisher Walter Hines Page "represented America in London during these trying years as no other Ambassador in London has ever represented us, with the exception of Charles Francis Adams during the Civil War." This service was so appreciated in England that the marriage of the ambassador's daughter gave King George V an opportunity to show his personal regard for Page. The king requested that the wedding be held, not in Westminster Abbey, but in the Royal Chapel of St. James's Palace. It was the first time that any marriage in which bride and bridegroom were foreigners had ever been celebrated in this centuries-old scene of royal weddings. The letter which Page wrote his daughter Katherine after the wedding couple had sailed for the United States is in marked contrast to the mood expressed by Prince Albert on page 63. The use below of Katherine's initials (her husband was a captain) was characteristic of Page's easy effervescence.

London, September 1, 1915

My Dear K.A.P.-tain:

You'll land to-morrow or next day—good; I congratulate you. Salute the good land for me and present my respectful compliments to vegetables that have taste and fruit that is not sour —to the sunshine, in fact, and to everything that ripens and sweetens in its glow.

And you're now (when this reaches you) fixing up your home—your *own* home, dear Kitty. Bless your dear life, you left a home here—wasn't it a good and nice one?—left it very lonely for the man who has loved you for twenty-four years and been made happy by your presence. But he'll love you twenty-five more and on and on—always. So you haven't lost that—nor can you. And it's very fit and right that you should build your own nest; that adds another happy home, you see. And I'm very sure it will be happy always. Whatever I can do to make it so, now or ever, you have only to say . . .

I laugh as I think of all your new aunts and cousins looking you over and wondering if you'll fit, and then saying to one another as they go to bed: "She is lovely—isn't she?" I could tell 'em a thing or two if I had a whack at 'em.

And you'll soon have all your pretty things in place in your pretty home, and a lot more that I haven't seen. I'll see 'em all before many years—and you, too! Tell me, did Chud get you a dinner book? Keep your record of things: you'll enjoy it in later years. And you'll have a nice time this autumn—your new kinsfolk, your new friends and old, and Boston and Cambridge . . .

My love to you, and Chud too,

Affectionately,
W. H. P.

*   *   *

*"I offer you the big things
of the whole world . . ."*

Jack London Makes a Last Ditch Stand to Gain His Child's Love:

His second marriage having embittered not only his first wife, but his daughters as well, Jack London—by that time author of *The Call of the Wild, The Sea Wolf* and many other stories—had failed to come to grips with some of the realities of life. When his younger daughter was fourteen, he tried to persuade her mother—humbling himself enough to appear at her house—to

7 3

permit the children to visit him at his large California ranch. He wanted them so much, he said, that he would change his will to favor the girls instead of his second wife; he would build a separate house for his first wife, so that she wouldn't have to deal with the second. But the first Mrs. London was intractable. Several days after his unsuccessful interview, the author wrote to his teen-age daughter:

[1919]

. . . Now, Joan, it is a hard proposition to put up to you at your age, and the chances are that in deciding on this proposition I put up to you on Sunday night you will make the mistake of deciding to be a little person in a little world. You will make that mistake because you listened to your mother, who is a little person in a little part of the world, and who, out of her female sex jealousy against another woman, has sacrificed your future for you. I offer you the big things of the whole world, the big things that big people live and know and think and act.

After a long silence, Joan answered in a one-page rejection. Because she and her sister were "pawns in a situation neither understood," as Joan put it in her biography of her father, they were unwilling to leave their mother. "Letters largely replaced visits and outings during the last years of his life when he spent little time in California, but it was through these, and because the girls were no longer children, that father and daughters finally came to know each other."

❋   ❋   ❋

"Anything you do is a further installment
on my indebtedness . . ."

Rabbi Stephen Wise Celebrates His Fiftieth Year in America:

Stephen Wise was brought to the United States from Hungary as the infant son of the new Rabbi of Temple Rodeph Sholom, New York, and the grandson of the chief rabbi in Hungary. He himself became not simply a rabbi, but a spokesman for his fellow Jews, and as a Zionist he lived to see the establishment of Israel. In this mercuric note he tells his son some of his feelings as an immigrant.

[Lake Placid, 1925]

Fifty years ago I landed—"I" the least because the youngest member of the expedition. I say today, for it is Tish-a-Bab [the anniversary of the destruction of ancient Jerusalem]. Imagine the joy of my parents. Grandma seeing my Father whom she adored and had not really seen since my birth, 16 months before. Otto cried, "Now that I have seen my father again, let me die" . . . Fancy, he was three years and seven months old, I one year and four months.

Fifty years ago! What years they were, if only my father had had more of them, and some years of leisured ease. I thank God for my Father's decision, and his and Grandma's courage in fighting on through the years. Not in a selfish spirit do I feel like "Bensching Gomel" [giving praise]. And I thank God for America—my parents' and ours and yours! And I have tried to repay my debt to America in part. Anything you and Justine will in the future do is to be a further installment on my indebtedness to America.

I thank God for the years and the memories, and most of all the larger life with Mother and our children, and for the glory that is to be—your child and Joan's!

*　　*　　*

*"I was rather afraid that you had thought
I was being hardhearted . . ."*

George VI to Princess Elizabeth After Her Marriage to Philip:

Because Philip Mountbatten was the first eligible young man the Princess had met, and because she had fallen in love with him when she was very young, King George had the average father's misgivings about her lack of contact with other young men. In 1944, the King had written his mother that "Philip had better not think any more about [marrying Elizabeth] for the present." He continued to withhold his consent for three years, but in 1947, after Elizabeth had been taken on a tour of South Africa by her parents, there no longer was doubt about the mutual affection of the two young people. The betrothal was announced in July, and Elizabeth and Philip were married on November 20, 1947. Not long afterward, while she was on her honeymoon, the royal bride received this touching expression of her father's feelings:

. . . I was so proud of you & thrilled at having you so close to me on our long walk in Westminster Abbey, but when I handed your hand to the Archbishop I felt I had lost something very precious. You were so calm & composed during the Service &

said your words with such conviction, that I knew everything was all right.

I am so glad you wrote & told Mummy that you think the long wait before your engagement & the long time before the wedding was for the best. I was rather afraid that you had thought I was being hardhearted about it. I was so anxious for you to come to South Africa as you know. Our family, us four, the 'Royal Family' must remain together with additions of course at suitable moments!! I have watched you grow up all these years with pride under the skilful direction of Mummy, who as you know is the most marvellous person in the World in my eyes, & I can, I know, always count on you, & now Philip, to help us in our work. Your leaving us has left a great blank in our lives but do remember that your old home is still yours & do come back to it as much & as often as possible. I can see that you are sublimely happy with Philip which is right but don't forget us is the wish of

> Your ever loving & devoted
> Papa.

III

* * *

The Great World

*. . . on the threshold of new
and separate lives . . . sometimes gratefully
received advice . . . on manners,
loyalties, tastes . . . on finding self . . .
and recognizing heritage . . .*

*"He will mine with the unseen
tunnels of his treachery . . ."*

A Roman Bishop Urges His Son to Avoid
Evil Company:

Apollinaris Sidonius, a fifth-century Roman born in Gaul, had
all the requisites for stunning success. He was a noble who had
been given the finest schooling, he married well, and he knew the
right people; his political career seemed assured. But the times
were full of pitfalls. Skeptical of Rome's waning power, Sidonius
played skilfully with Theodoric II, the Visigothic king, and might
have seized the privilege he coveted had not his father-in-law
become Emperor of the West. Unfortunately for Sidonius, the
new emperor was soon assassinated, and the ambitious son-in-law
fled back to Gaul to begin a new series of intrigues. He had been
Prefect of Rome, then Patrician, but he never satisfied his great
desire to be named Consul; while the Empire collapsed around
him, he ended his days as bishop of the old Gallic town of Arverna.
This letter on manners was written to his son Apollinaris when
Sidonius's star was still in ascendancy.

[*c.* A.D. 469]
The love of purity which leads you to shun the company
of the immodest has my whole approval; I rejoice at it and respect it, expecially when the men you shun are those whose ap-
titude for scenting and retailing scandals leaves nothing privi-
leged or sacred, wretches who think themselves enormously
facetious when they violate the public sense of shame by shameless language. Hear now from my lips that the standard-bearer
of the vile troop is the very Gnatho of our country. Imagine an
arch-stringer of tales, arch-fabricator of false charges, arch-re-

tailer of insinuations. A fellow whose talk is at once without end and without point; a buffoon without charm in gaiety; a bully who dares not stand his ground. Inquisitive without insight, and three-times more the boor for his brazen affectation of fine manners. A creature of the present hour, with ever a carping word ready for the past and a sneer for the future. When he is after some advantage, no beggar so importunate as he; when refused, none so bitter in depreciation. Grant his request and he grumbles, using every artifice to get better terms; he moans and groans when called on to refund a debt, and if he pays, you never hear the end of it. But when anyone wants a loan of him he lies about his means and pretends he has not the wherewithal; if he does lend, he makes capital out of the loan, and bruits the secret abroad; if debtors delay repayment he resorts to calumny; when they have absolved the debt he tries to deny receipt.

Abstinence is his abomination, he loves the table; but a man who lives well wins no praise from him unless he treats well too. Personally he is avarice itself; the best of bread is not for his digestion unless it is also the bread of others. He only eats at home if he can pilfer his viands, and send them off amid a storm of buffets. He cannot indeed be wholly denied the virtue of frugality; he fasts when he cannot get himself invited. Yet with the light perversity of the parasite, he will often excuse himself when asked; on the other hand, if he sees that men avoid him, he will fish for invitations. If left out he grows abusive; if admitted, unbearably elate: no blow descends upon him unexpected. If dinner is served late, he falls like a bandit upon the dishes; if appetite is stilled too soon, he falls to lamentation. Thirst unquenched makes him quarrelsome, drunkenness makes him sick.

If he banters others, he grows scurrilous; if others banter

him, ungovernable; take him for all in all, he is like the filth in sewers, the fouler the more you stir it. His life brings pleasure to few, love to none, contemptuous mockery to all. He is one to burst bladders or break canes upon, one whose thirst for drink is only excelled by his thirst for scandal; exhaling loathsomeness, frothing wine, uttering venom, he makes one doubt for what to hate him most, his unsavoriness, his drunken habits, or his villany. "But," you may say, "perhaps a fair complexion lends a color to a vile nature; perhaps his charm of person redeems ineptitude of mind; the man may have elegance or exquisite taste; he may create a good impression on those who meet him."

In point of fact, his person is fouler and more unsightly than a corpse rolled half-burnt from the pyre when the brands have settled—such a thing as a very undertaker's slave could not bring himself to put back. He hardly sees out of his eyes, which, like the Stygian lake, roll waters down through darkness. His ears are elephantine; an ulcered skin surrounds each aperture with indurated waste, either helic is bossed with suppurating tumors. His nose is broad at the nostrils and narrow at the bridge, strait for his own olfactory ends, but for the spectator a cavernous vision of horror. He obtrudes a face with leaden lips and a bestial rictus, with purulent gums and brown teeth, enhanced by eructations from the feast of yesterday and the bilges of his excesses at the board. A forehead too he flaunts hideous with creases and distensions of the brows. He grows a beard which age vainly whitens, since Sylla's malady keeps it black. His whole face is as pale as if it were ever dolorous with infesting shades. I spare you the hulking residue, gout-ridden, flat and flabby. I spare you his weal-furrowed skull, covered with almost as many scars as hairs. I spare you the description of a nape so short that when his head is thrown back it seems to merge into his shoulder blades.

The sunken carriage, the lost grace and vigor of his arms, the gouty hands bound cestus-like with greasy poultices; all these I spare you, so too the hircine armpits that entrench his sides, and polute the air for every nostril near him with a reek three times more pestilent than that from Ampsanctus' cave. And breasts collapsed with adiposity horrible on a man's body even in mere protuberance, but now hanging like a mother's. And the pendulous folds of the abdomen about genitals thrice shameful in their debility, a foul creased covering worse than what it hides. Why should I tell of his back and spine? True, the ribs do sweep round from the vertebral joints and cover the chest, but the whole branching structure of bones is drowned under a billowing main of belly. I pass over the fat reins and buttocks which make even his paunch look insignificant in comparison. I pass the bent and withered thigh, the swollen knees, the slender hams, the horny shanks, the weak ankles, the small toes and enormous feet.

As I have drawn him, he is horrible enough in his deformity, a monster from whom his infinite noisomeness drains half the blood and life, who cannot sit a litter or walk a yard, however much they prop him. But his tongue is more detestable still than his other members. He keeps it busy in the service of the vilest prurience; but is most dangerous of all to patrons with anything to hide. For those in luck he belauds, but to those who are unfortunate he betrays; let a tempting moment but urge to disclosure of a friend's secret, and instantly this Spartacus will break all bars and open every seal. He will mine with the unseen tunnels of his treachery the houses which the rams of open war have failed to breach. This is the fashion in which our Daedalus crowns the edifice of his friendships, sticking as close as Theseus in prosperity; but when adversity comes, more elusive than any Proteus. The more you avoid even a first introduction to such company the better you will please me; especially to those so shameless that they talk like degraded players at the booths, and know neither bar nor bridle. For when a man exults in leaving all seemliness and decency behind, and fouls a loose tongue with the dirt of all lawless licences, be sure his heart is no less filthy than his language. You may find an evil liver with a serious tongue; the foul tongue and virtuous life are rarely allied. Farewell.

*　　*　　*

". . . as far as father may and can,
I charge you . . ."

The Duke of Suffolk Bids Farewell to His Eight-Year-Old Heir:

William de la Pole, Duke of Suffolk, assumed his title when his brother was killed at Agincourt, and became a valiant general in England's wars with France. It was he who arranged the marriage of the weak-minded Henry VI to Margaret of Anjou and thereby brought upon himself an unhappy fate. He was impeached for bartering the province of Maine to France in return for Margaret's hand. In an effort to save him from the angry Yorkist faction, the King sent Suffolk into five-years exile. This letter to Suffolk's young son John was written on the eve of his departure.

[April 30, 1450]

My dear and only well-beloved son, I beseech Our Lord in Heaven, the maker of all the world, to bless you, and to send you ever grace to love Him and to dread Him; to the which, as far as a father may charge his child, I both charge you, and pray you to set all your spirits and wits to do, and to know His holy laws and commandments, by which ye shall, and with His great mercy, pass all the great tempests and troubles of this wretched world.

And that also, wittingly, ye do nothing for love nor dread of any earthly creature that should displease Him. And there as any frailty maketh you to fall, beseech His mercy soon to call you to Him again with repentance, satisfaction, and contrition of your heart, never more in will to offend Him.

Secondly, next Him above all earthly things, to be true liegeman in heart, in will, in thought, in deed, unto the King our aldermost high and dread sovereign lord, to whom both ye and I be so much bound to; charging you, as father can and may, rather to die than to be contrary, or to know anything that were against the welfare or prosperity of his most royal person, but that as far as your body and life may stretch ye live and die to defend it, and to let his Highness have knowledge thereof in all the haste ye can.

Thirdly, in the same wise, I charge you, my dear son, alway, as ye be bounden by the commandment of God to do, to love, to worship, your lady and mother; and also that ye obey alway her commandments, and to believe her counsels and advices in all your works, the which dread not but shall be best and truest to you. And if any other body would steer you to the contrary, to flee the counsel in any wise, for ye shall find it naught and evil.

Furthermore, as far as father may and can, I charge you in any wise to flee the company and counsel of proud men, of covetous men, and of flattering men, the more especially and mightily to withstand them, and not to draw nor to meddle with them, with all your might and power. And to draw to you and your company good and virtuous men, and such as be of good conversation, and of truth, and by them shall ye never be deceived nor repent you of.

Moreover, never follow your own wit in no wise, but in all your works, of such folks as I write above, ask your advice and counsel; and doing thus, with the mercy of God, ye shall do right well, and live in right much worship, and great heart's rest and ease.

And I will be to you as good lord and father as my heart can think.

And last of all, as heartily and as lovingly as ever father blessed his child in earth, I give you the blessing of Our Lord and of me, which of his infinite mercy increase you in all virtue and good living. And that your blood may by His grace from kindred to kindred multiplying in this earth to His service, in such wise as after the departing from this wretched world here, ye and they may glorify Him eternally amongst His angels in Heaven.

Written of mine hand,
     the day of my departing fro this land,
          Your true and loving father,
          Suffolk

"We now see an instance of the fearful state of indiscipline into which England was drifting," says Sir Winston Churchill in *The Birth of Britain*. "When the banished Duke was crossing the Channel with his attendants and treasure in two small vessels, the *Nicholas of the Tower,* the largest warship in the Royal Navy, bore down upon him and carried him on board. He was received by the captain with the ominous words 'Welcome, traitor,' and two days later he was lowered into a boat and beheaded by six strokes of a rusty sword. It is a revealing sign of the times that a royal ship should seize and execute a royal Minister who was travelling under the King's special protection." Left fatherless, the son of the murdered duke could scarcely have disregarded the letter above more flagrantly. Instead of being a "true liegeman" to King Henry, John de la Pole married the sister of Edward IV, who deposed Henry. Indeed, John lived very comfortably among his father's foes.

*   *   *

"You need not bring much
shift of clothes . . ."

A Father's Letter Intercepted in Mary Stuart's Prison:

During her long stay in prison, the Queen of Scots had with her a youngster named Bess Pierrepont who was Mary's goddaughter and on whom the queen lavished the motherly affection she was not permitted to give her son, the boy-king of Scotland. Young Bess came to the royal prisoner when she was four, and when she was sixteen, she fell in love with Jacques Nau, the queen's secretary, a man more than twice her age. Perhaps it was this attachment which caused the teen-ager to be so carefully watched, but it is more likely that suspicion was based on her father's prominence as a Catholic in Protestant England. Though Sir Henry Pierrepont could not have written a more innocuous letter than this one to his daughter, it was not construed as such by Mary's jailer, who refused to deliver it. Sir Henry was "a peevish Papist," an offense that denied his daughter even the knowledge that he had written to her. Yet where is there offense in these lines?

With God's hearty blessings from your mother and me, we both being desirous to see you before we go up, the rather, for that upon some respects (which at your coming hither we will acquaint you withal) we do break up house, and know not when we shall come so near you again, do most humbly beseech the Queen's Majesty, your mistress, to give you leave to come over for two or three days; and in hope of that favour, I have sent my servants to wait on you. You need not bring much shift of clothes with you, because of your short abode here, and therefore I have sent no trunk, but only a mail for your night stuff. I pray you present my humble duty to the Queen's Majesty your mistress (wherein your mother desireth, for her part, to be remembered). And so, with my humble commendations to Mr. Nau, my son, Curle, and the rest of my good friends in your company, commit you to God his good protection.

At Woodhouse, the 7th of April 1585.

> Your loving father,
> H. Pierrepont

Your mother desireth you to do her very hearty commendations unto Mr. Nau and your good man.

Sir Henry's offense was described by Queen Mary's jailer in a letter to his superiors in London: "It was a shame for [Bess] to be nourished and brought up here in Popery as she is, and that if

[Pierrepont] had sent for her, to keep her still at home, I could have been content to let her come unto him; but sending for her to return hither again in two or three days, he showed himself to be a *fole* . . ."

*   *   *

". . . the best profit and return
will be this . . ."

Walter Raleigh Tells His Son to Be Cautious in Friendship:

Under sentence of death for thirteen years, Sir Walter secured his release from the Tower of London by promising James I that he could find a gold mine in Guiana without encroaching on Spanish claims. The ensuing expedition included his son Walter, who was killed in a fight with the Spanish on the banks of the Orinoco River. So enraged was Raleigh at the loss of his son that the recriminations he heaped upon the youth's commanding officer caused the latter to kill himself. In an era of intemperate reprisal, Raleigh was a shrewd and ruthless critic of loyalties of every kind. Here is his advice to his son on friendship:

Above all things, be not made an ass to carry the burdens of other men: if any friend desire thee to be his surety, give him a part of what thou hast to spare; if he presses thee further, he is not thy friend at all, for friendship rather chooseth harm to itself than offereth it. If thou be bound for a stranger, thou art a fool; if for a merchant, thou puttest thy estate to learn to swim; if for a churchman, he hath no inheritance; if for a lawyer, he will find an invasion by a syllable or word to abuse thee; if for a poor man, thou must pay it thyself; if for a rich man, he needs not; therefore from suretyship, as from a manslayer or enchanter, bless thyself; for the best profit and return will be this, that if thou force him for whom thou art bound, to pay it himself, he will become thy enemy; if thou use to pay it thyself, thou will be a beggar.

Raleigh was not always so sternly prudent. He was hard put to report their son's death to Lady Raleigh. "I was loathe to write," he said, "because I knew not how to comfort you; and God knows, I never knew what sorrow was until now. All that I can say to you is, that you must obey the will and providence of God; and remember that the Queen's Majesty bore the loss of Prince Henry with a magnanimous heart . . . . comfort your heart, dearest Bess, I shall sorrow for us both. . . . My brains are broken and it is a torment for me to write, and especially of misery."

*   *   *

> *"I had rather you should be*
> *Charles le bon, than le grand . . ."*

Charles I Gives His Creed of Kingship to the Prince of Wales:

Charles Stuart's fate had not yet been sealed, but he knew "not how far God may permit the malice and cruelty of my enemies to proceed" when he wrote these "reflections of my conscience" for his son—who was not to become Charles II until eleven years after his father's execution. The first Charles had at least the average man's love for his wife and children, but he believed in his divine right as a monarch and would not bend to meet the needs of his subjects. He was articulate enough in passing on these precepts to his heir. He was no great scholar, but he was a remarkable connoisseur of paintings; his interest in literature was such that during his captivity he read the sermons of Launcelot Andrews, Hooker's *Ecclesiastical Polity*, Spenser's *Faerie Queen* and Shakespeare. Piety and an earnest dedication to monarchy mark this testament written for the eighteen-year-old prince.

SON: If these papers, with some others, wherein I have set down the private reflections of my conscience, and my most impartial thoughts, touching the chief passages which have been most remarkable, or disputed in my late troubles, come to your hands, to whom they are chiefly designed, they may be so far useful to you, as to state your judgement aright in what hath passed; whereof a pious use is the best can be made; and they may also give you some directions how to remedy the present distempers, and prevent (if God will) the like for time to come. . . .

I had rather you should be Charles *le bon*, than *le grand*, good, than great; I hope God hath designed you to be both; having so early put you into that exercise of His grace and gifts bestowed upon you, which may best weed out all vicious inclinations, and dispose you to those princely endowments and employments, which will most gain the love, and intend the welfare of those over whom God shall place you. . . .

Above all, I would have you, as I hope you are already, well grounded and settled in your religion, the best profession of which I have ever esteemed that of the Church of England, in which you have been educated; yet I would have your own judgement and reason now sealed to that sacred bond which education hath written, that it may be judiciously your own religion, and not other men's custom or tradition which you progress. . . .

Take heed of abetting any factions, or applying to any public discriminations in matters of religion, contrary to what is in your judgement and the churches well settled; your partial adhering as head to any one side gains you not so great advantage in some men's hearts (who are prone to be of their King's religion) as it loseth you in others; who thinks themselves and their profession first despised, then persecuted by you; take such a course as may either with calmness and charity quite remove the seeming differences and offences by impartiality, or so order affairs in point of power that you shall not need to fear or flatter any faction.

For, if you ever stand in need of them, or must stand to their courtesy, you are undone. The serpent will devour the dove; you may never expect less of loyalty, justice, or humanity than from those who engage in religious rebellions; their interest is always made God's, under the clours of piety, ambitious policies march, not only with the greatest security, but applause as to the populace; you may hear from them Jacob's voice, but you shall feel they have Esau's hands. . . .

Never charge your head with such a crown as shall, by its heaviness, oppress the whole body, the weakness of whose parts cannot return anything of strength, honour, or safety to the head, but a necessary debilitation and ruin.

Your prerogative is best showed and exercised in remitting rather than exacting the rigour of the laws; there being nothing worse than legal tyranny.

In these two points of preservation or established religion and laws, I may (without vanity) turn the reproach of my sufferings, as to the world's censure, into the honour of a kingdom of martyrdom, as to the testimony of my own conscience; the troubles of my kingdoms, having nothing else to object against me but this, that I prefer religion and laws established before those alterations they propounded. . . .

It is all I have now left to me, a power to forgive those that have deprived me of all; and I thank God I have a heart to do it, and joy as much in this grace, which God hath give me, as in all my former enjoyments; for this is a greater argument of God's love to me than any prosperity can be. Be confident (as I am) that the most of all sides, who have done amiss, have done so, not out of malice, but misinformation, or misapprehension of things. . . .

As your quality sets you beyond any duel with any subject, so the nobleness of your mind must raise you above the meditating any revenge, or executing your anger upon the many. . . .

If God shall see fit to restore me, and you after me, to those enjoyments which the laws have assigned us, and no subjects, without an high degree of guilt and sin can divest us of; then may I have better opportunity when I shall be so happy to see you in peace, to let you more fully understand the things that belong to God's glory, your own honour, and the kingdom's peace.

But if you never see my face again, and God will have me buried in such a barbarous imprisonment and obscurity (which the perfecting some men's designs requires) wherein few hearts that love me are permitted to exchange a word or a look with me, I do require and entreat you as your father and your King, that you never suffer your heart to receive the least check against or disaffection from the true religion established in the church of England. . . .

When they have destroyed me (for I know not how far God may permit the malice and cruelty of my enemies to proceed, and such apprehensions of some men's words and actions have already given me) as I doubt not my blood will cry aloud for vengeance to Heaven; so I beseech God not to pour out His wrath upon the generality of the people who have either deserted me, or engaged me, through the artifice and hypocrisy of their leaders, whose inward horror will be their first tormentor, nor will they escape exemplary judgements. . . .

And if God will have disloyalty perfected by my destruction, let my memory ever, with my name, live in you; as of your father, that loves you, and once a King of three flourishing kingdoms; whom God thought fit to honour, not only with the sceptre and government of them, but also with the suffering many indignities and an untimely death for them; while I studied to preserve the rights of the Church, the power of the laws, the honour of my crown, the privileges of Parliaments, the liberties of my people and my own conscience, which I thank God, is dearer to me than a thousand kingdoms.

I know God can—I hope he will—restore me to my rights. I cannot despair, either of His mercy, or my people's love and pity.

At worst, I trust I shall but go before you to a better kingdom, which God hath prepared for me, and me for it, through my Saviour Jesus Christ, to whose mercy I commend you, and all mine.

Farewell, till we meet, if not on earth, yet in Heaven.

*　　*　　*

Catherine the Great Is Instructed
in the Behavior of a Wife:

A comet streaked across the dark Latvian night as the carriage bearing an obscure fourteen-year-old German princess and her ambitious mother pressed on towards St. Petersburg. To Sophie Auguste Fredericke of Zerbst, soon (because of the intrigues of Frederick the Great) to be Catherine of Russia, the comet was real and unforgettable. Not so the letter the girl had been given by her father, Prince Christian August. She dutifully thanked him for his "gracious instructions," and promptly put them out of her mind. Catherine's parent had made his letter as formal as possible, addressing her in the third person in an effort to underscore the rigidity of the obligations his daughter must assume as the consort of a Russian crown prince.

[February 1744]

To Princess Sophie Auguste Fredericke.

Next to the Empress, her Majesty, she has to respect the Grand Duke above all as her Lord, Father, and Sovereign; and withal to win by care and tenderness at every opportunity his confidence and love. Her Lord and His will are to be preferred to all the pleasures and treasures of the world; and do nothing which he dislikes or which cause him only a little pain; and still less to insist on her own will.

Never to enter into familiarity or badinage, but always have respect as much as possible.

To regard the domestics and favorites of her Lord with a gracious mien; not to demand the services of her Lord but ever to respond to the favor and love of her Lord.

To speak with no one alone in the audience chamber and to conduct herself always according to etiquette there.

To detest and avoid playing cards for high stakes, which is a mark of avarice and self-interest.

To take charge herself of the pocket money which may be given her, to guard it and pay it out gradually to a servant on an account, in order that she may not submit herself to the trusteeship of a governess; to employ it for her use and her pleasure, and with it to do good, in order that she may win for herself and not for others instead of her the love and inclination of her dependents.

To intercede for no one, because one may not understand the laws and a one-sided report cannot be trusted, and the side discriminated against becomes a disgruntled enemy; and he whom one helps out with such intercessions forgets the good deed and goes and sins again.

Especially to enter into no affairs of government in order not to irritate the Senate.

Four months after her husband became Czar Peter III, Catherine entered into the affairs of government as head of a conspiracy. Two months later, she was Russia's sole sovereign.

* * *

Diderot, in Prison, Reads a Lecture from His Estranged Father:

In the summer of 1749, Louis XV of France had Denis Diderot thrown into the dungeon of Vincennes for his anti-religious writings. The thirty-five-year-old philosopher had balked consistently at his father's ambitions for him, and only recently had started work on the monumental *Encyclopaedia* which was to cause the wrath of all the authorities in which the elder Diderot believed. Yet the young man needed his father's approbation. When he was moved from solitary confinement to a room in which he could write, he immediately dashed off a letter to his parent. Within a fortnight he received the following stern response:

Langres, September 3, 1749

My son,

I have received the two letters which you wrote me recently, informing me of your detention and its cause.

But I cannot help saying that there absolutely must have been other reasons aside from the ones given in one of your letters, for your being put between four walls.

Everything coming from the Sovereign is respectable and must be obeyed. . . .

But since nothing happens without God's consent, I do not know which is better for your moral well-being: that the imprisonment which you have had in that pebble-box should be ended, or that it should be prolonged for several months during which you could reflect seriously on yourself.

Remember, that if the Lord has given you talents, it was

not for you to work to weaken the doctrines of our Holy Religion, which you must certainly have attacked for such a large number of ecclesiastical persons to protest against one of your works, or, at least, against those that are imputed to you.

Until then, I have given you sufficient proof of my love. In giving you an education, it was in the hope that you would make good use of it and not that its results should throw me, as they have done, into the most bitter sorrow and chagrin, on learning of your disgrace. . . .

Forgive, and I shall forgive you.

I know, my son, that no one is exempt from calumny, and that they may impute to you works in which you have had no share.

But to give proofs of the contrary to the influential people whom you know, give to the public some Christian production of yours which will free your pen of all contrary thoughts they may have concerning it, I mean about your way of thinking.

This work will bring you the blessings of Heaven, and will keep you in my good graces. However I warn you that you will never receive any consideration, from me until you have informed me, truly and unequivocally, whether you are married, as they have written to me from Paris, and whether you have two children. If this marriage is legitimate and the thing is done, I am satisfied. I hope you will not refuse your sister the pleasure of bringing them up, and me the pleasure of seeing them under my own eyes.

You ask for money.

What!

A man like you who is working on immense projects, as you are, can need money?

And you have just spent a month in a place where it cost you nothing to live!

Besides I know that his Majesty, out of his kindness, gives an honorable sustenance to those who, as a result of his orders, are placed where you are.

You have asked me to send you paper, pens and ink. I invite you to make better use of them than in the past.

Remember the memory of your poor mother. In the reproaches that she made to you, she told you several times that you were blind. Give me proofs to the contrary. Once again, and above all, be faithful in the execution of your promises.

You will find enclosed a draft for one hundred and fifty *livres* on the account of Maître Foucou which you will spend as you see fit.

I await impatiently the happy day which will calm my worries by informing me that you are free.

As soon as I find out I shall go and render thanks to the Lord.

Meanwhile, my son, with all the love that I owe you.

Your affectionate father,
Diderot

It was not until two months later that the prison gates opened for Diderot—perhaps because Jean-Jacques Rousseau wrote so passionately to Madame Pompadour, pleading either to have Diderot released or to be incarcerated with him. Father and son were reconciled in 1752, when Diderot finally admitted that he had indeed been married for nine years.

*　　*　　*

Diderot Describes a Newly Discovered
Prescription to His Daughter:

The marriage which so concerned his father when Diderot was in prison was charged with discord. The young philosopher had chosen a wife of whom he once complained: "Her inflexibility, her ill-humor . . . is visibly killing me, herself and her sister." Yet the marriage lasted. In old age he wrote that he had a wife "who cherishes me, for whom will she scold when I am no longer here?" Three years before his death he wrote to his daughter, telling her of a way he had found to put her mother in good humor.

[July 1781]

. . . She bought a copy of *Gil Blas* to restore to Mlle Goyet the one you lost. While waiting for the opportunity to return it, she began to read it, and enjoyed it; and I saw that it was reflected in her whole day. Consequently I have become her reader; three pinches of *Gil Blas* every day, one in the morning, one in the afternoon, one at night. When we come to the end of *Gil Blas,* we shall try the *Limping Devil,* the *Bachelor of Salamanca* and other gay works of that kind. . . . The funniest thing is that she regales all her visitors with what she remembers, and thus conversation doubles the efficaciousness of the remedy.

I had always thought of novels as frivolous productions, but finally I have discovered that they are good for vapors; I shall indicate the prescription to Dr. Tronchin the next time I see him. Recipe eight to ten pages of the *Comic Novel;* four chapters of *Don Quixote;* a carefully chosen paragraph of Rabelais; make an infusion of the whole business in a reasonable quantity of *Jacques the Fatalist* or *Manon Lescaut;* and vary these drugs as you vary medicinal herbs, substituting others having approximately the same virtue.

Though *Gil Blas* may have cheered Madame Diderot, it did not stop her scolding. After her husband suffered a severe stroke, she admonished him because he insisted upon eating an apricot. "How the devil can it hurt me?" he asked her, downing the fruit Still defying her, he reached for some cherries. Then, as his wife looked at him, he died.

*　　*　　*

'. . . big with secrets they do not know."

Lord Chesterfield Discusses a Few Rules of Business:

In 1728, Philip Stanhope, Lord Chesterfield, was sent to Holland as ambassador. There, four years later, was born to him, by a certain Mademoiselle du Bouchet, a natural son who was named for his father. Chesterfield had great hopes for the child and, over a period of twenty-one years, wrote him hundreds of letters charged sometimes with wit, sometimes with urgent and heart-felt advice. The lad was nineteen and on his first business venture in Paris when he received the following:

London, December 19, O.S. 1751

My dear Friend,

You are now entered upon a scene of business, where I hope you will one day make a figure. . . . Business does not exclude (as possibly you wish it did) the usual terms of politeness and good-breeding, but, on the contrary, strictly requires them. . . . Be upon your guard against the pedantry and affectation of business, which young people are apt to fall into, from the pride of being concerned in it too young. They look thoughtful, complain of the weight of business, throw out mysterious hints, and seem big with secrets which they do not know. Do you on the contrary never talk of business but to those with whom you are to transact it; and learn to seem *vacuous* and idle when you have the most business. Of all things, the *volto sciolto* and the *pensieri stretti* are necessary. Adieu!

The young Philip Stanhope completely disregarded his father's precepts, and his death at the age of thirty-six brought overwhelming grief to Lord Chesterfield, who discovered only then that his son had long been married to a woman of humble origin. The widow, Eugenia, further humiliated her father-in-law by publishing his letters without permission. Having no children by his wife (the illegitimate daughter of George I), Chesterfield sought solace for the loss of young Stanhope by adopting his godson who thereafter was also known as Philip Stanhope.

*　　*　　*

Leopold Mozart Takes His *Wunderkind* to Task for His Impulsive Ways:

The young Mozart is said once to have cried, "Next after God, Papa!" His vain old father had so managed his son's genius that by the time Mozart was fourteen he had been fawned over by most of Europe's royalty, and had been invested by the pope as a *cavaliere* of the order of the Golden Spur. But it is torturous for most prodigies to grow up. Mozart bridled at the treatment given him by the Archbishop of Salzburg to whose court he was attached. Wilfully, against his father's weak-kneed instincts, Mozart set out at twenty-two for Paris, where he had been received ecstatically as the *Wunderkind* in 1763. Sadly, he discovered that a talented young man was not considered as much of a sensation as a precocious child, and he made his feelings known to his father, who responded in character:

[1778]

MY SON! You are hot-tempered and impulsive in all your ways! Since your childhood and boyhood your whole character has changed. As a child and a boy you were serious rather than childish, and when you sat at the clavier or were otherwise intent on music, no one dared to make the slightest jest. Why, even your expression was so solemn that, observing the early efflorescence of your talent and your ever grave and thoughtful little face, many discerning people of different countries sadly doubted whether your life would be a long one. But now, as far as I can see, you are much too ready to retort in a bantering tone to the first challenge—and that, of course, is the first step toward undue familiarity, which anyone who wants to preserve his self-respect will try to avoid in this world. A goodhearted fellow is inclined, it is true, to express himself freely and naturally; nonetheless it is a mistake to do so. And it is just your good heart which prevents you from detecting any shortcomings in a person who showers praises on you, has a great opinion of you and flatters you to the skies, and who makes you give him all your confidence and affection; whereas as a boy you were so extraordinarily modest that you used to weep when people praised you overmuch. The greatest art of all is *to know oneself* and then, my dear son, to do as I do, that is *to endeavour to get to know others through and through.* This, as you know, has always been my study; and certainly it is a fine, useful and indeed most necessary one. As for your giving lessons in Paris, you need not bother your head about it. *In the first place,* no one is going to dismiss his master at once and engage you. *In the second place,* no one would dare to ask you, and you yourself would certainly not take on anyone except possibly some lady who is already a good player and wants to take lessons in interpretation, which would be easy work for good pay. For instance, would you not have gladly undertaken to give Countess von Lützow and Countess Lodron two or three lessons a week at a fee of two or three louis d'or a month, the more so as such ladies also put themselves to much trouble to collect subscribers for the engraving of your compositions? In Paris everything is done by these great ladies, many of whom are devoted lovers of the clavier and in some cases excellent performers. These are the people who can help you. As for composition, why, you could make money and gain a great reputation by publishing *works for the clavier, string quartets, and so forth, symphonies* and possibly a collection of *melodious French arias* with clavier accompaniments like the one you sent me, and finally operas. Well, what objection have you to raise now? But you want everything to be done at once, before people have even seen you or heard any of your works. Read my long list of the acquaintances we had in Paris at that time. All, or at least most of them, are the leading people in that city and they will all be both delighted and interested to see you again. Even if only six of them take you up (and indeed one single one of the most influential of them would be enough), you would be able to do whatever you pleased.

The Paris excursion was a failure, and Mozart returned to spend two more years in the service of the haughty Archbishop of Salzburg. Finally, the conditions imposed on him became so intolerable that he submitted his resignation, making the mistake—as his father saw it—of "expressing himself freely and naturally." It is said that the Archbishop had him evicted bodily.

*   *   *

"For Heaven's sake . . . do not part
with your heart too rapidly . . ."

Dr. Burney Urges His Daughter Fanny
to Reject M. D'Arblay:

The famous Fanny Burney—confidante of Dr. Johnson, Mrs. Thrale, Madame de Staël and dozens of others—was forty-one when the letter below was written. Her father was as famous as she. Dr. Charles Burney had spent twenty years on his *History of Music,* enjoying the patronage of Edmund Burke and Charles James Fox; Fanny's *Evelina* was a work of fiction that had opened to her (at the age of twenty-six) doors to the literary figures she considered more important than politicians. She adored her father, but coveted independence, too. In 1792, she encountered a group of French exiles, cast adrift by the unpredictable swirls of the French Revolution, and soon she was wholly enamoured of the adjutant-general to Lafayette—a man "open as the day—warmly affectionate to his friends—intelligent, ready, and," she told her diary, "amusing in conversation, with a great share of *gaieté de coeur,* and, at the same time, of *naïveté* and *bonne foi.*" Fanny

May 1793

Dear Fanny—I have for some time seen very plainly that you are *éprise,* and have been extremely uneasy at the discovery. You must have observed my silent gravity, surpassing that of mere illness and its consequent low spirits. I had some thoughts of writing to Susan about it, and intended begging her to do what I must now do for myself—that is, beg, warn, and admonish you not to entangle yourself in a wild and romantic attachment, which offers nothing in prospect but poverty and distress, with future inconvenience and unhappiness. M. d'Arblay is certainly a very amiable and accomplished man, and of great military abilities I take for granted; but what employment has he for them of which the success is not extremely hazardous? His property, whatever it was, has been confiscated—décrété—by the Convention; and if a counter-revolution takes place, unless it is to be exactly such a one as suits the particular political sect in which he enlisted, it does not seem likely to secure him an establishment in France. And as to an establishment in England, I know the difficulty which very deserving natives find in procuring one, with every appearance of interest, friends, and probability; and, to a foreigner, I fear the difficulty will be more than doubled.

As M. d'Arblay is at present circumstanced, an alliance with anything but a fortune sufficient for the support of himself and partner would be very imprudent. He is a mere soldier of fortune, under great disadvantages. Your income, if it was as certain as a freehold estate, is insufficient for the purpose; and if the Queen should be displeased and withdraw her allowance, what could you do?

I own that, if M. d'Arblay had an establishment in France sufficient for him to marry a wife with little or no fortune, much as I am inclined to honour and esteem him, I would wish to prevent you from fixing your residence there; not merely from selfishness, but for your own sake. I know your love for your family, and know that it is reciprocal; I therefore cannot help thinking that you would mutually be a loss to each other. The friends, too, which you have here, are of the highest and most desirable class. To quit them, in order to make new friendships in a strange land, in which the generality of inhabitants at present seem incapable of such virtues as friendship is built upon, seems wild and visionary.

If M. d'Arblay had a sufficient establishment here for the purposes of credit and comfort, and determined to settle here for life, I should certainly think ourselves honoured by his alliance; but his situation is at present so very remote from all that can satisfy prudence, or reconcile to an affectionate father the idea of a serious attachment, that I tremble for your heart and future happiness. M. d'Arblay must have lived too long in the great world to accommodate himself contentedly to a little; his fate seems so intimately connected with that of his miserable country, and that country seems a greater distance from peace, order, and tranquility now than it has done at any time since the revolution.

These considerations, and the uncertainty of what party

will finally prevail, make me tremble for you both. You see, by what I have said, that my objections are not personal, but wholly prudential. For Heaven's sake, my dear Fanny, do not part with your heart too rapidly, or involve yourself in deep engagements which it will be difficult to dissolve; and to the last degree imprudent, as things are at present circumstanced, to fulfil.

As far as character, merit, and misfortune demand esteem and regard, you may be sure that M. d'Arblay will always be received by me with the utmost attention and respect; but, in the present situation of things, I can by no means think I ought to encourage (blind and ignorant as I am of all but his misfortunes) a serious and solemn union with one whose unhappiness would be a reproach to the facility and inconsiderateness of a most affectionate father.

Dr. Burney's letter did not move his daughter. "M. d'Arblay," she wrote in her diary, "is one of the most singularly interesting characters that can ever have been formed. He has a sincerity, a frankness, an ingenuous openness of nature, that I had been unjust enough to think could not belong to a Frenchman." He was also without a sous. The only income available to these middle-aged lovers was from a pension of £100 allotted by the Queen of England to Fanny because of her five years' service as Keeper of Robes, and £20 in an annuity made possible by the success of her novel *Cecilia*. Unabashed, Fanny Burney became Madame d'Arblay in July, 1793, and she continued to write, with financial reward, for the rest of her life. Though frequently beset by poverty, the marriage was a continuing love story.

*　　*　　*

Sir Walter Scott Has Some Thrifty Words for a Soldier Son:

Scott said of his elder son: "My own selfish wish would have been that he should have followed the law; but he really had no vocation that way, wanting the acuteness and liveliness of intellect indispensable to making a figure in that profession. He has chosen a profession for which he is well suited, being of a calm but remarkably firm temper—fond of mathematics, engineering and all sorts of calculation—clear-headed and good natured. When you add to this a good person and good manners, with great dexterity in horsemanship and all athletic exercises, and a strong constitution, one hopes you have the grounds of a good soldier." The younger Scott had recently been appointed a cornet in the 18th Hussars and was stationed in Corke when his father wrote:

Abbotsford 4 Septr. [1819]

Dear Walter—Your very acceptable letter of the 26th reached me today. . . . Respecting the allowance Colonel Murray informs me that from £200 to £250 in addition to the pay of a cornet ought to make a young man very comfortable. He adds which I am pleased to hear that your officers are manys of them men of moderate fortune and disposed to be œconomical. I had thought of £200 as what would suit us both but when I see the account which you very properly keep I will be better able to determine. It must be considered that any uncommon expence as the loss of a horse or the like may occasion an extra draught over and above the allowance—I like very much your methodical arrangement of expences: it is rather a tiresome thing at first to keep an accompt of pounds shillings and pence but it is highly necessary and enables one to see how the money actually goes.

It is besides a good practical way of keeping up acquaintance with arithmetic and you will soon find the principles on which all military movements turn are arithmetical and that though one may no doubt learn to do them by rote yet *to understand* you must have recourse to numbers. Your adjutant will explain this to you. By the way as he is a foreigner you will have an opportunity to keep up a little of your French and German. Both are highly necessary to you. The knowledge of the last with a few other qualifications made several officers' fortunes last war. . . .

. . . As you Hussars smoke I will give you one of my pipes. But you must let me know how I can send it safely. It is a very handsome one though not my best. I will keep my *Meerschaum* untill I make my continental tour and then you shall have that also. I hope you will get leave for a few months and go with me. Yours ever affectionately

Walter Scott

✳   ✳   ✳

A Nineteenth Century Father Considers
the Hazards of a Daughter's Debut:

William Frend, who spent half his life in the eighteenth century, and in a variety of occupations, did not become a father until he was fifty-two. Eventually he settled down as actuary of the Rock Insurance Company. His daughter Sophia was born in 1809, and on the occasion of her first dance her over-age father was moved to write the wise, witty and youthful letter that follows:

[*circa* 1825]

My dear Sophia,

Your letter is of too much importance for me to wait for a frank.[2] Your mother does not object to your going to the ball; I may add that I not only do not object, but approve of it, as you go in a party in whom I can place the utmost confidence. It is rather too soon for you to go to such places, which are neither to be eagerly sought after, nor to be fastidiously rejected. Though I was early initiated into the mysteries of dancing, and by a residence in France, before I went to College, acquired a somewhat greater skill in capering than the generality of young men of my age, yet I did not go to a ball, except in vacation times in the country, till I had taken my first degree. Young as you are, yet I can trust you in a ball-room without any fears of your being guilty of impropriety; yet there are a few things worth your knowing, and some against which you should be on your guard. The main point is to avoid affectation of every kind,

[2] An envelope bearing a signature entitling a letter to free postage.

whether in walk, gesture, or talk. In the common modes of dancing you have had instruction enough, and of them I say nothing. Anything like romping in dancing is to be carefully avoided. There is a certain distance to be moved over in a given time. I have seen girls scurrying through twice that distance, and thinking they had done a great feat; but, in fact, they only made themselves ridiculous, and looked like hoydens. Mind your time and the figure of the dance, and should you ever in the latter be set right by your neighbour, take it in good part, and be sure you make him or her sensible you feel obliged to them. I perceive by your letter that you already have two partners, but should you have any other, which I don't object to, don't stand like a statue, but converse with him freely, if he is so inclined; but beware of making any remark that is to the disadvantage of any person in the room. Use your eyes well; look about you and notice those who appear to be the most graceful in their gestures and manner of conversation. You may probably have some people of rank there, ladies who discredit by their rude, dashing behaviour, and others who do credit to their station by propriety of conduct. There is an awkward bashfulness and a bold look of self-importance, between which is the happy medium which distinguishes a well-bred woman. Few are there that can make either a good bow or a good curtsey. I care not whether it is a low one, as in my time, or a nod, or a slip, as is now the fashion; there is grace in doing either, which, if you cannot attain, still the extreme may be avoided. Observe what is done by others, but avoid imitation; what may be graceful in one may not suit another. Each has a suitable modification peculiar to himself which, if it is changed by affectation, makes him ridiculous. The great secret, however, is to carry with you a cheerful and innocent heart, desirous of giving and receiving all the satisfaction which the amusement is capable of affording, wishing no ill to your neighbours, passing over their faults, and highly regarding their excellences. Though the eyes of many may be upon you, yet you are to act as if no one regarded you, careful only that what you are about you do as well as you can. I shall be glad to hear your remarks on the first exhibition of the kind that you have been at.

William Frend had the esteem and the warm affection of a large circle of literary and scientific people, including Lady Byron, whom he helped to establish a village school. His letters to his daughter have the same tone as those to his distinguished friends. Once he wrote Sophia: "A King of Siam told an English traveller that he was uttering a falsehood, because he said in his country the rivers became so hard that an elephant might walk over them. Numbers of people are in the same situation as the King of Siam."

✳   ✳   ✳

*"I wonder at our great men
who introduce foreign customs . . ."*

Noah Webster Finds Little to Please in a White House Dinner:

The first edition of Noah Webster's *American Dictionary* had been published when he went to Washington to use his influence in behalf of a law to protect authors through copyright. "My presence here," he wrote to his son-in-law, William Fowler, "has, I believe, been very useful and perhaps necessary to the accomplishment of the object." But in writing to his daughter, Fowler's wife, he was more concerned with passing foibles of official Washington.

Washington, D.C., December 29, 1830.

My Dear Harriet W,

I have been here more than a fortnight promoting the passage of a law extending the rights of authors. I was confined for ten days with a violent cold or influenza, but am now in good health . . .

Yesterday I called on the President [Andrew Jackson], introduced by Mr. Grundy of Tennesee, who is a lodger with us. The President asked me to dine with him, and I could not well avoid it. We sat down at 6 o'clock and rose at 8. The President was very sociable and placed me, as a stranger, at his right hand. The party, mostly members of the two houses, consisted of about thirty. The table was garnished with artificial flowers placed in gilt urns, supported by female figures, on gilt waiters. "We had a great variety of dishes, French and Italian cooking. I do not know the names of one of them. I wonder at our great men who introduce foreign customs, to the great annoyance of American guests. To avoid annoyance as much as possible, the practice is to dine at home and go to the President's to see and be seen, to talk and to nibble fruit, and to drink very good wines. As to *dining* at the President's table in the true sense of the word, there is no such thing." (The foregoing paragraph in commas might well appear in the prints, but the writer must not be known.)

I rejoice most gratefully that Mr. Fowler has recovered.

Give my love and respect to him, and tell little Emily [Webster's granddaughter] I do not forget her, but love her as much as ever. Respects to all friends.

With sincere affection,
N. Webster

✳   ✳   ✳

". . . it will be pretty sure to come out . . ."

Coventry Patmore, at Sixteen, Gets His Father's Advice on Writing:

Peter George Patmore was a writer whose only work of art was his son Coventry. A close friend of William Hazlitt [p. 17], the elder Patmore was described by another friend as "a person of rare intellectual endowments and a companion in whose society it was impossible to pass a dull hour." He was also a dedicated father who wanted most of all to see that his son's talent found its true direction. He sent Coventry to study French in Saint-Germain when he was sixteen, and it was during this period that the boy became seriously interested in writing poetry. When he turned to his father for advice he received the following:

London, Oct. 31, 1839.

My dear Coventry,

. . . I am quite satisfied with the style and *composition* of your letter and you therefore have no occasion to be dissatisfied with them. The only exception to this is, that you do not punctuate—and consequently that you give the *appearance* (but nowhere the reality) of running your sentences into one another —simply for want of the *full stop* and the capital letter which in every case follow.

. . . Touching poetry—if you have any of it in you it will be pretty sure to come out—whether you will or no—but do not *entice* it out—for of all the follies there is none so foolish in its results as the habit of mere *verse*-writing. There is no harm in the Charivari man's phrenological prognostic about your head. [A Paris phrenologist had advised Coventry to consider himself a poet.] But if there is anything in it (in the prognostic I mean) or if you think there is anything in it—it is a reason the more for eschewing verse-making: for I verily believe there never yet was a *poetical* genius that was not cursed rather than blessed by the possession—unless it was Shakespeare.

Bye-the-bye, you never tell me what you do in Paris when you go there—whether you stay there all day—whether you *dine* (or merely call) at the "Place" [Place Vendôme where lived an English girl by whom Coventry was smitten]—if not, *where* and *how* you dine, etc. Not that I am anxious about your proceedings at the "Place"—but (shall I say it) I am rather anxious. And this not much from what you say, as from what you do *not* say. Whenever Telemachus was *silent* to his mentor, there was always some cause for fear to both. Do not suppose that I (your mentor—if you will let me be so) have any fear that the "Place" should prove to you a Calypso's Island. But it may prove a more dangerous place—a Prospero's Island—without a Prospero to watch over the welfare of its inhabitants. You will tell me in reply that it is indeed a place

"full of sweet airs
That give delight and hurt not"

and that its Miranda *is* a Miranda—and what would I desire more? Yes—my dear little boy—but you are not a Ferdinand. But (again you reply) can evil come out of good? Yes—the greatest evils out of the greatest goods—always understanding the axiom of now—middle of the 19th Century. Still, be assured, no evil can come to you even out of evil, much less out of good, while you lay bare all your thoughts and feelings to *me*, and listen to mine in return, as those of one who would fain be to you a Mentor and a Ulysses in one.

I never preach to you, and never shall: though I am by no means sure that I may not some day or other—if you should happen to be cast away on an enchanted island like that of Calypso, and wish to take up your abode there—watch an opportunity of inveigling you to the top of a convenient cliff, and push you into the sea, jump in after you, at the imminent peril of both our precious lives: which is more than Mentor did for his Telemachus—for, being an immortal, he knew that there was no danger for either of them.

Although P. G. Patmore never successfully managed his own life, his mentorship helped his son to achieve a distinguished place among Victorian poets. "I have written very little," Coventry Patmore said, "but it is all my best; I have never spoken when I had nothing to say, nor spared time or labour to make my words true. I have respected posterity; and should there be a posterity which cares for letters, I dare hope that it will respect me."

*   *   *

Sam Houston Instructs a Soldier in His Duty to His Native Soil:

After thirty years in Texas, during which he had won the war that made it an independent nation, served as President of the Republic, then as senator for thirteen years, Sam Houston was Governor of the Lone Star State when the Civil War broke out. Though he was a Southerner through and through (he had been Governor of Tennessee before going west), he believed in the Union and Texan loyalty to it. But this was a battle that Houston lost. When the state voted to secede, he refused to swear allegiance to the Confederacy, and in March, 1861, he was declared deposed. Sam Houston, Jr., was in a training camp when he received this declaration of his father's point of view:

Cedar Point, 23rd July 1861.

. . .

I had hoped, my dear son, that in retirement my mind would be engrossed, so far as I am concerned with affairs of the times, in the cares of my Domestic circle and matters concerning my family alone, and that I could live in peace. In the train of events now transpiring, I think I perceive disasters to Texas. The men and arms are leaving this quarter of the theatre in the great Drama, which is playing, and is to be played. I know not how much statesmanship Lincoln may have, or Generalship at his command, and therefore I would not be wise to Prophesy. But looking at matters as they seem to me, his wise course, I would say is, that Texas is his great point in which to make a lodgment and thereby make a diversion from the seat of war. Texas in his possession, and the Gulf is his with Fort Pickens as

119

a convenient Point. The assault upon Texas will require two armies & weaken the army of Eastern operations. If Texas is attacked she must be in her present isolated condition. She can look for no aid from the Confederacy and must either succumb or defend herself. Are our means sufficient to do this? What is her situation as has been represented by the newspapers? Has she arms, men, ammunition, in an emergency to defend herself? Arkansas is crying for help. Our frontier is again assailed by the Indians, and she will be left alone in these straits and without means. Missouri must yield to the pressure by which she is surrounded. The States of Illinois, Iowa, Indiana, Minnesota, Nebraska, must be overrun, and then Texas must be the Ultimate Point in the campaign of subjugation and spoil. Under the circumstances, is it wise for her to send, unasked and at the instigation of "Major Marshall," her men and arms? That wretch has been a botch on humanity and will be a scab on Texas. I am ready, as I have ever been, to die for my country, but to die without a hope of benefit by my death is not my wish. The well-being of my country is the salvation of my family; But to see it surrendered to Lincoln, as sheep in shambles, is terrible to me.

I fear that within twenty days, or less, an assault will be made upon some part of our coast, and how are we prepared to repel it? Have we men? Will we have means? Our troops, with leaders, have never been beaten, and with good ones, they will always be invincible. Will Major Marshall, McLeod, Sherman, or the gallant men made by the Convention, or the Committees of vigilance, save us in an hour of peril? Does anyone suppose that proclamations by a Clark will save the Country in the hour of her peril; yet no one else has power but those to whom I have referred! The fact that a park of flying artillery is on the vessel now in our harbor is proof that a landing is designed somewhere on the coast. The question arises: is it wise to send our men and arms at the instance of Major Marshall!

These matters, my son, I have written to you, and have to say in conclusion, if Texas did not require your services, and you wished to go elsewhere, why then all would be well, but as she will need your aid, your first allegiance is due to her and let nothing cause you in a moment of ardor to assume any obligation to any other partner whatever, without my consent. If Texas demands your services or your life, in her cause, stand by her.

Houston is not, nor will be a favorite name in the Confederacy! Thus you had best keep your duty and hopes together, and when the Drill is over, come home. Your Dear Ma and all of us send best love to you and Martin. Give my regards to General Rogers, Colonel Daly, & Dr. Smith, when will you be home, my son! Thy Devoted Father,

Sam Houston

Sam Houston, Jr.

*   *   *

" . . . not so old as you . . . when I first had to win my food . . ."

Dickens Sends His Youngest Son into the World of Men:

Dickens had seven sons and he wanted each to find his own answer to life. One was in India, one in South America and one in Australia when, in September, 1868, the youngest boy, Edward Bulwer Lytton Dickens, sixteen, left home for good. "Poor Plorn is gone to Australia," Dickens wrote a friend. "It was a hard parting at the last. He seemed to become once more my youngest and favorite little child as the day drew near, and I did not think I could have been so shaken." Dickens left his office in the Strand and handed the letter below to his son as Plorn boarded the boat train.

My dearest Plorn,

I write this note to-day because your going away is much upon my mind, and because I want you to have a few parting words from me to think of now and then at quiet times. I need not tell you that I love you dearly, and am very, very sorry in my heart to part with you. But this life is half made up of partings, and these pains must be borne. It is my comfort and sincere conviction that you are going to try the life for which you are best fitted. I think its freedom and wildness more suited to you than any experiment in study or office would ever have been; and without that training, you could have followed no other suitable occupation.

What you have already wanted until now has been a set, steady, constant purpose. I therefore exhort you to persevere in a thorough determination to do whatever you have to do as well as you can do it. I was not so old as you are now when I first had to win my food, and to do this out of determination, and I have never slackened in it since.

Never take a mean advantage of anyone in any transaction, and never be hard upon people who are in your power. Try to do to others, as you would have them do to you, and do not be discouraged if they fail sometimes. It is much better for you that they should fail in obeying the greatest rule laid down by your Saviour, than that you should.

I put a New Testament among your books, for the very same reason, and with the very same hopes that made me write an easy account of it for you, when you were a little child; because it is the best book that ever was or ever will be known in the world, and because it teaches you the best lessons by which any human creature who tries to be truthful and faithful to duty can possibly be guided. As your brothers have gone away, one by one, I have written to each such words as I am now writing to you, and entreated them all to guide themselves by this book, putting aside the interpretations and inventions of men.

You will remember that you have never at home been wearied about religious observances or mere formalities. I have always been anxious not to weary my children with such things before they are old enough to form opinions respecting them. You will therefore understand the better that I now must solemnly impress upon you the truth and beauty of the Christian religion, as it came from Christ Himself, and the impossibility of your going far wrong if you humbly but heartily respect it.

Only one thing more in this head. The more we are in earnest as to feeling it, the less we are disposed to hold forth about it. Never abandon the wholesome practise of saying your own private prayers, night and morning. I have never abandoned it myself, and I know the comfort of it.

I hope you will always be able to say in after life, that you had a kind father. You cannot show your affection for him so well, or make him so happy, as by doing your duty.

Your affectionate Father.

When the train pulled out with his son on board, Dickens went to his club and described the event to his daughter: "I can honestly report that he went away, poor fellow, as well as could possibly be expected. He was pale, and had been crying, and

(Harry said) had broken down in the railway carriage after leaving Higham station; but only for a short time.

Just before the train started he cried a good deal, but not painfully. (Tell Georgy that I bought him his cigars.) These are hard, hard things, but they might have to be done without means or influence, and then they would be far harder. God bless him!"

The day before, however, Dickens had written to a friend complaining of the expense of buying Plorn's outfit and sending Harry to Cambridge at the same time. "I can't get my hat on in consequence of the extent to which my hair stands on end at the costs and charges of these boys. Why was I ever a father! Why was my father ever a father!"

✳   ✳   ✳

*"I am nearly toothless
and in my second childhood."*

Dr. Livingstone Describes the Heart of Africa and Its Effects:

The famous encounter with Henry Morton Stanley was yet to come when David Livingstone stopped to write letters at a jungle outpost, not knowing when, if ever, he would be able to send them. One of the longest was to his son Tom, aged twenty, and living in England, where he had recently met with an accident.

Town of Moenékuss, Manyuema Country
24th September, 1869

My dear Tom,—I begin a letter, though I have no prospect of being able to send it off for many months to come. It is to have something in readiness when the hurry usual in preparing a mail does arrive. I am in the Manyuema Country, about 150 miles west of Ujiji, and at the town of Moenékoos, or Moenékuss, a principal chief among the reputed cannibals. His name means 'Lord of the light grey parrot with a red tail,' which abounds here, and he points away still further west to the country of the real cannibals. His people laugh and say 'Yes, we eat the flesh of men,' and should they see the inquirer to be credulous enter into particulars. A black stuff smeared on the cheeks is the sign of mourning, and they told one of my people who believes all they say that it is animal charcoal made of the bones of relatives they have eaten. They showed him the skull of one recently devoured, and he pointed it out to me in triumph. It was the skull of a gorilla, here called 'soko,' and this they do eat. They put a bunch of bananas in his way, and hide until he comes to take them, and spear him. Many of the Arabs believe firmly in the cannibal propensity of the Manyuema. Others who have lived long among them, and are themselves three-fourths African blood, deny it. I suspect that this idea must go into oblivion with those of people who have no knowledge of fire, of the Supreme Being, or of language. The country abounds in food, —goats, sheep, fowls, buffaloes, and elephants: maize, holcserghum, cassaba, sweet potatoes, and other farinaceous eatables, and with ground-nuts, palm-oil, palms and other fat-yielding nuts, bananas, plantains, sugarcane in great plenty. So there is little inducement to eat men, but I wait for further evidence.

Not knowing how your head has fared, I sometimes feel greatly distressed about you, and if I could be of any use I would leave my work unfinished to aid you. But you will have every medical assistance that can be rendered, and I cease not to beg the Lord who healeth His people to be gracious to your infirmity.

The object of my expedition is the discovery of the sources of the Nile. Had I known all the hardships, toil, and time involved I would have been of the mind of Saint Mungo of Glasgow, of whom the song says that he let the Molendinar Burn 'rin by' to Egypt, and never made 'drumly' by my plashing through them. But I shall make this country and people better known. 'This,' Professor Owen said to me, 'is the first step; the rest will follow in due time.' . . .

The examination of the water shed contained the true scientific mode of procedure, and Sir Roderick said to me: 'You will be the discoverer of the sources of the Nile.' I shaped my course for a path across the north end of Lake Nyassa, but to avoid the certainty of seeing all my attendants bolting at the first sight of the wild tribes there, the Nindi, I changed off to go round the south end, and if not, cross the middle. What I feared for the north took place in the south when the Johanna men heard of the Mazitu, though we were 150 miles from the maurauders, and I offered to go due west till past their beat. They were terrified, and ran away as soon as they saw my face turned west. I got carriers from village to village, and got on nicely with people who had never engaged in the slave-trade; but it was slow work. I came very near the Mazitu three times, but obtained information in time to avoid them. Once we were taken for the Mazitu ourselves, and surrounded by a crowd of excited savages. They produced a state of confusion and terror, and men fled hither and thither with the fear of death on them. Casembe would not let me go into his southern district till he had sent men to see that the Mazitu, or, as they are called in Lunda, the Watuta, had left. Where they had been all the food was swept off, and we suffered cruel hunger. We had goods to buy with, but the people had nothing to sell, and were living on herbs and mushrooms. I had to feel every step of the way, and generally was groping in the dark. No one ever knew anything beyond his own district, and who cared where the river ran? Casembe said, when I was going to Lake Bangweolo: 'One piece of water was just like another (it is the Bangweolo water), but as your chief desired you to visit that one, go to it. If you see a traveling party going north, join it. If not, come back to me and I will send you safely along my path by Moero'; and gave me a man's load of fish like whitebait. I gradually gained more light on the country, and slowly and surely saw the problem of the fountains of the Nile developing before my eyes. The vast volume of water draining away to the north made me conjecture that I had been working at the sources of the Congo too. My present trip to Manyuema proves that all goes to the river of Egypt. In fact, the headwaters of the Nile are gathered into two or three arms, very much as was depicted by Ptolemy in the second century of our era. What we moderns can claim is rediscovery of what had fallen into oblivion, like the circumnavigation of Africa by the Phoenician admiral of one of the Pharaohs B.C. 600. He was not believed, because 'he had the sun on his right hand in going round from east to west.' Though to us this stamps his tale as genuine, Ptolemy was not believed, because his sources were between 10 and 12 north latitude, and collected into two or three great head branches. In my opinion his informant must have visited them.

I cared nothing for money and contemplated spending my life as a hard-working poor missionary. By going into the country beyond Kuruman we pleased the Directors, but the praises they bestowed excited envy. Mamma and you all had hard times. The missionaries at Kuruman, and south of it, had comfortable houses and gardens. They could raise wheat, pumpkins, maize, at very small expense, and their gardens yielded besides apples, pears, apricots, peaches, quinces, oranges, grapes, almonds, walnuts, and all vegetables, for little more than the trouble of watering. A series of drouths compelled us to send for nearly all our food 270 miles off. Instead of help we had to pay the uttermost farthing for everything, and got bitter envy besides. Many have thought that I was inflated by the praises I had lavished upon me, but I made it a rule never to read anything of praise. I am thankful that a kind Providence has enabled me to do what will reflect honour upon my children, and show myself a stout hearted servant of Him from whom comes every gift. None of you must become mean, craven-hearted, untruthful or dishonest, for if you do, you don't inherit it from me. I hope that you have selected a profession that suits your taste. It will make you hold up your head among men, and is your most serious duty. I shall not live long, and it will not be well to rely on my influence. I could help you a little while living, but have little else than what people call a great name to bequeath afterwards. I am nearly toothless and in my second childhood. The green maize was in one part the only food we could get with any taste. I ate the hard fare, and was once horrified by finding most of my teeth loose. They never fastened again, and generally became so loose as to cause pain. I had to extract them, and did so by putting on a strong thread with what the sailors call a clovehitch, tie the other end to a stump above or below, as the tooth was upper or lower, strike the thread with a heavy pistol or stick, and the tooth dangled at the stump, and no pain was felt. Two upper front teeth are thus out, and so many more, I shall need a whole set of artificials. I may here add that the Manyuema stole the bodies of slaves which were buried, till a threat was used. They said the hyenas had exhumed the dead, but a slave was cast out by the Banyamwezi, and neither hyenas nor men touched it for seven days. The threat was effectual. I think that they are cannibals, but not ostentatiously so. The disgust expressed by native traders has made them ashamed. Women never partook of human flesh. Eating sokos or gorillas must have been a step in the process of teaching them to eat men. The sight of a soko nauseates me. He is so hideously ugly, I can conceive of no other use for him than sitting for a portrait of Satan. I have lost many months by rains, refusal of my attendants to go into a canoe, and irritable eating ulcers on my feet from wading in mud instead of sailing. They are frightfully common, and often kill slaves. I am recovering, and hope to go down Lualaba, which I would call Webb River or Lake; touch then another Lualaba, which I will name Young's River or Lake; and then by the good hand of our Father above turn homewards through Karagwe. As ivory trading here is like gold-digging, I felt constrained to offer a handsome sum of money and goods to my friend Mohamed Bogharib for men. It was better to do this than go back to Ujiji, and then come over the whole 260 miles. I could have waited there for men from Zanzibar, but the authority at Ujiji behaved so oddly about my letters, I fear they never went to the coast. The worthless slaves I have saw that I was at their mercy, for no Manyuema will go into the next district, and they behaved as low savages who have been made free alone can. Their eagerness to enslave and kill their own countrymen is distressing.

Give my love to Oswell and Anna Mary and the Aunties. I have received no letter from any of you since I left home. The good Lord bless you all, and be gracious to you.—Affectionately yours,

David Livingstone

The great African explorer was on his last expedition when he wrote this letter. Not until March, 1871, did he reach the Lualaba River, and in October he had found his way back for a brief respite at Ujiji, on the eastern shore of Lake Tanganyika. Here it was that Henry M. Stanley finally caught up with him. "I pushed back the crowds," Stanley wrote, "and, passing from the rear, walked down a living avenue of people, until I came in front of the semicircle of Arabs, in front of which stood the white man with the grey beard. As I advanced slowly towards him I noticed he was pale, looked wearied, had a grey beard, wore a bluish cap with a faded gold band around it, had on a red-sleeved waist-coat, and a pair of grey tweed trousers. I would have run to him, only I was a coward in the presence of such a mob—would have embraced him, only, he being an Englishman, I did not know how he would receive me. So I did what cowardice and false pride suggested was the best thing—walked deliberately to him, took off my hat, and said: 'Dr. Livingstone, I presume?'

" 'Yes,' said he, with a kind smile, lifting his cap slightly."

* * *

". . . these people think one is made of stone . . ."

George V Suggests the Prince of Wales Find More Time for Himself:

The young man who was to become Edward VIII and finally the Duke of Windsor was off on the first of his good-will tours of the British Empire when the letter below was written. He was only twenty-five, but his charm and sincerity made him an ideal ambassador, and he was to spend much of his youth in this capacity.

130

That his talents were appreciated is more than clear in these words of his father:

Buckingham Palace
Oct 12th/19

Dearest David
　. . . You might take things easier during the last month of your visit & give yourself more spare time & get more rest from the everlasting functions & speeches which get on one's nerves. I warned you what it would be like, these people think one is made of stone & that one can go on forever; you ought to have put your foot down at the beginning & refused to do so much. . . . All I wish to say now is that I offer you my warmest congratulations on the splendid success of your tour, which is due in great measure to your own personality & the wonderful way in which you have played up. It makes me very proud of you & makes me feel very happy that my son should be received with such marvellous enthusiasms of loyalty and affection. I have had many letters from all sorts of people in Canada, as well as members of yr. Staff all singing yr. praises. . . .

Ever my dear boy
Yr. most devoted Papa
G. R. I.

＊　　＊　　＊

Sherwood Anderson Looks at the Influence
of His Generation on That of His Son:

The familiar story of Sherwood Anderson's defection from the management of a paint business in favor of life as a struggling writer changed, as it was bound to, the lives of his three children. Though there were long separations, and three stepmothers, the bond between father and child was never broken. His sons grew up seeking his advice and getting it in remarkably candid letters. In the following letter, Sherwood Anderson is writing to Robert Lane Anderson, who succeeded his father as editor and publisher of two weekly newspapers in Marion, Virginia.

Richmond, Virginia [November, 1929]

Dear Bob: I am comfortably placed here at the Westmoreland Club, not at all expensive. They put me in a tiny room, but I am moving this afternoon to a large room on the second floor where there is a good-sized room in which to work.

It seems a bit silly of me sometimes, not to be there with you, but this whole thing has done me good.

I think what happened to me was rather strange and amusing.

I guess you do not know, and perhaps never will know, the underlying basic difference between your generation and mine. In my generation, as you know—you kids of mine had partly to pay for it—I was a rebel.

Could there be anything more strange than what has happened to me?

I wanted for people, quite frankly, many things my generation did not have. I fought for it in my life and work.

Then the War came. The War did more than anything I or my kind could have done to make people face life.

For example, the old battleground was sex. That led naturally to an emphasis on sex. We all saw, everyone saw, the effect of repressions.

I and my kind told the story of repressed life. I have never thought of myself as a profound thinker. I was the storyteller; I took my color from the life about me. You know that for a long time after I began writing I was condemned on all sides. That is pretty much forgotten now. My *Winesburg, Ohio,* was condemned as a sex-server. How strange that notion seems now.

And then came the Great War. Never mind what the War was. It was terrific in its physical aspects—bodies mangled, the young manhood of England, Germany and France blown away or bled white, a great nation like Germany humiliated in the end.

Never mind all that. That is past.

But something else got blown up in that war too: the repressions, the strange fear of sex, the resultant underestimate of life. The young men who went into it got, must have got, a profound sense of life's cheapness.

You, my son, did not get into the war. You were too young. You just escaped it. Just the same you are not at all the man you would have been but for the War.

Of course there came other forces at work—the flowering of the industrial age, speeded up, no doubt, by the War.

Thousand[s] of men, everywhere, jerked out of the old individualistic life—plenty of machinery to jerk them out fast, machinery to kill them in masses like cattle—hurled into a new mass life.

The old individualist—the man of the pre-War period, who

was a young man then, who got his sharp impressions then (most of us continue all our lives to live in the impressions of youth; the men, the young men who got their sharp impressions of life in the War will probably continue to live in those impressions the rest of their lives)—the old individualist type of man—well, you see now where he was.

Why talk of sex repressions now? Apparently there aren't any.

I remember, son, a certain woman who fought long and bitterly for woman's suffrage. The women got what they fought for.

But this particular woman couldn't quit fighting for woman suffrage. She kept right on. One day I was walking with a young woman, and we saw this older woman. As she knew me, she stopped. "What are you doing now?" I asked.

She began again on the rights of women. They had got some things but not enough. The words she was saying would have been glowing words twenty years ago. I shall never forget the puzzled look in the younger woman's eyes. She was a post War kid. "Rights of women? What the devil is the old girl talking about?" she asked.

Well, you see where I am, son—or at least have been these last five years. I had a world, and it slipped away from me. The war blew up more than the bodies of men, as I have already suggested.

It blew ideas away——

Love

God

Romance.

I am working on a book. I call it *No God*. I could just as well call it *No Love*. It is not without significance that Gauguin is your favorite modern painter while my favorite is Van Gogh. I remember what Gauguin said of love. "If I were to say the word, it would crack the teeth out of my mouth," he said.

As regards this transition, this sweeping change that has come in the whole underlying conceptions of life, it is a profound one.

If I were a bit older, it would not make any difference to me. The old are old.

As a man, as a writer, I had to ask myself which road I wanted to take. I could simply have been old, not to have tried to understand you and your brother and sister.

I fought against you for a long time. Who has cried out more sharply than myself against the coming of industrialism, the death of individualism, the modern world?

Well, I have already told the story of the man crying in the wilderness. I have been going about for four or five years now saying to myself, "To hell with that."

I want to say to you now that I would very likely have lost this little private battle of mine, that concerns no one vitally but myself, but for you kids of mine.

It would have meant kindly tolerance on your part, "The old man's all right." You know, that sort of thing.

In *No God*, the novel on which I am now at work, I am telling the story of man having his roots in the pre-War life, accepting the present day post-War life.

That is my man's story. He is a man who has had marriage in the old way—memories of it cling to him—and then he comes to accept a woman who is a product of the new world.

No God—No Love—in the old sense. That is what it means.

As for the woman, well, I see her every day on the street. I've a notion that she doesn't want and wouldn't take what men used to give women, calling it love. I hope I am right about her. She is the young female kid of today. She has had sex experience and will have more, when she wants it.

I look at her as my man in the book *No God* looks at her— glad of her, certainly all for her.

Writing about her and of my man's acceptance of her is fun. It is refreshing. It is good for me.

There is certainly plenty of the old pre-War thing in men, the fear of the new life that has constantly to be put down.

No God was the tentative title of a novel that Anderson abandoned before publication, but the search for meaning in human relationships never left him. Less than a year before his death in 1941, he said in a letter to his son John, a painter, ". . . I find this same problem exists in all fathers and sons. There is something about the relationship that is pretty difficult to put your finger on. I think fathers realize this and have it on their minds a good deal more than the sons realize. If you later have sons of your own, you may be up against the same problems one of these days . . . it may be true of all relationships, not only between fathers and sons, but between men and women. Nothing seems fixed. Everything is always changing. We seem to have very little control over our emotional life. . . ."

* * *

Sir Granville Bantock Describes the
British Scene to an Absent Son:

The climate of Great Britain in the 'twenties is reflected in several ways in this letter from the composer of *Omar Khayyam* and the *Hebridean Symphony*. Granville Bantock was—as he shows below—a great champion of competition festivals for the musical *hoi polloi*, but his heart was clearly not with the masses during the abortive nine-day General Strike of 1926—nor, indeed, does he seem enthusiastic about the beautiful Irish rebel, Maud Gonne. His report was written on the day the strike ended, to his son Raymond in Japan.

Buxton, May 12, 1926

My dear old Boy,

Your letter of April 6th I found awaiting me on my return home from Ireland last saturday, by the last and only Mail boat that was run during the week. We were glad to hear of your safe return to Japan after your adventurous wanderings, and we are already beginning to count the months that are to pass before you return home.

I left home at 9 A.M., and after changing trains at Derby, and again at Miller's Dale, and then getting a lift in a car to Buxton, arrived here at 3 P.M., to learn that the General Strike has petered out and been called off. There was no other possible course. The Trades Union Council never expected such an effective resistance. The country has been solid behind Baldwin and the Government kept cool and took effective measures to guard against panic and to protect the people. It was good to see the University students driving the omnibus and motor lorries with a bobby on every bus, and in Bham alone over 20,000 men were enrolled as special constables. Angus joined up and went on duty, while Ham was taken on by the Midland Railway at Saltley to get up steam and fire the engines ready for journeys. He was lodged in their barracks under police protection. Beyond wrecking the Flying Scotsmen Express, the strikers were able to do nothing, and had they tried rioting, I fancy they would have got much the worst of it. So much for the strike, which might have become a Revolution but for the firmness of Baldwin.

I am glad to hear that you enjoyed Sean O'Casey's play *Juno and the Paycock*. I have seen it acted 5 or 6 times, and enjoy it more each time. When in Dublin last week, I saw O'Casey's new play *The Plough and the Stars* at the Abbey Theatre, and met all the players in the Green Room, with Yeats and Lennox Robinson. It is a play dealing with the Irish Rebellion, and is a splendid piece of realism, though hardly equal to *Juno* in greatness. On the Monday night previous, Mrs. Despurd, Maud Gonne, Mrs. Sheffington and other irreconcilables stood outside the Abbey Theatre, and let off some stink-bombs inside as a protest on behalf of the Irish martyrs. They were promptly locked up by the Free State Government. I saw AE twice, and had tea with him at his home on Sunday. We went over his play of *Deirdre*, which I shall tackle as a Folk Opera, as soon as I have scored *The Song of Songs*. He was much interested to hear about you, and has given me another picture. The *Feis* was a great success as you will gather from the copies of *The Irish Times* which I sent you from Dublin. This week, I am adjudicating at the Buxton Festival for the 4th time—on Thursday, Friday and Saturday, and will spend Sunday with some friends at Alderley Edge, where I am adjudicating next year. These Festivals are a godsend, and I shall be away now each week-end until July. . . .

Sybil Thorndike has asked me to write the music for her production of *Macbeth* at Xmas, and I am very tempted to see what I can do. The play is my favourite, and I have an idea of using only brass instruments with Oboes and Bassoons (no strings at all) to express the savage barbarism that might shock the nerves of the stolid B. P. I am going to talk the matter over with her and her husband, Lewis Casson, when I am next in London or when they are in N. Wales for their holiday in the summer. Your time-table of work amazes me, and I wonder how you succeed in getting so much done. Now that your play is finished, you will be able to get some articles or stories written, which I hope may bring you in something.

I am much looking forward to reading your review of Claudel's *Tête d'Or*. It will be a very valuable experience for you, if you can return by Siberia, and visit Tashkent, Samarkand and other Russian centres en route, especially if you can get introductions from the Russion Council at Tokyo or Soviet representatives at Vladivostok and Harbin, where you seem to have made several good friends.

Well, I must get to work. Your new photo snapshot was very welcome. You are looking very well and younger.

Much love, dear boy, from

> Your ever affectionate
> Daddy

*   *   *

William Allen White Reports the Perils of Prohibition When Abroad:

Perhaps the most famous of all American country newspaper editors, William Allen White was appointed in 1930 by President Hoover to serve on a commission delegated to investigate the occupation of Haiti by United States troops. Always the reporter, White described his Haitian adventure to many correspondents. This account is to his son, W. L. White, then a young man working on his father's *Emporia Gazette*.

March 3, 1930

Dear Bill:

Of all the places I have ever been this is the most curious and interesting, and in some ways is the most important thing I have had to do. . . .

I saw a curious thing at the Governor's reception the other night—a man about forty or fifty, a dark swarthy mulatto, suddenly flashed across my face as the living spitting image of Charlie Curtis [Vice President of the United States] as he was thirty years ago. I never saw such a remarkable resemblance; the way he held his head, his physical mannerisms, his bodily form, his eyes, his mustache, his cheekbones, which we think in Curtis are North American Indian—all are just as marked in this man. . . . I noticed even his complexion is like that of Curtis. Somewhere back in the sixteenth or seventeenth century, maybe the early eighteenth, when Louis Papin, Curtis's grandfather, left France, he probably left a brother, or a cousin, or a grandfather and the old grandfather had more breeding vigor than a whiteface bull because there it is—the French of Curtis and the French of this man breeding through two races true to form in this generation. . . .

I have been with [the ruling elite in Haiti] a good deal, in their homes, at their clubs, and the other night I went to a country club dance. . . . I never saw such manners in my life; three kinds of wine on the buffet side table and nobody taking more than a few tablespoonsful occasionally in a little glass. I had the devil's own time because we commissioners are officially on the waterwagon, we drink nothing—at least all abstain publicly and so far as I know privately except purely ceremonial champagne—and I had to explain to these people why we do not drink wine being officials of a dry government. Of course I do not smoke and, of course, I do not dance, and I had to convince them that I was an ungodly liar, and I fear I left them with the suspicion that my other vice was wife-beating. But they were too subtle and sophisticated to show their disapproval, if they had it. But they must have thought I was a strange bird. . . .

The whole population feels that its liberties have been trampled down. They honestly feel that we are tyrannical, and the fact that the occupation is honestly trying to serve the Haitians does not get to them, because we are not serving them in the Haitian way. However, we are trying to serve them after the manner of American civilization and American ideas, which they loathe. We are in the 20th century looking toward the 21st. They are in the 18th century—with the ideals of the Grand Louis always behind them as models. We are pointing the way for them to enter the modern world. They love the old regime.

Write me the news of city politics. . . .

*   *   *

William Carlos Williams Considers His Son's Approach to Adulthood and Compares It with His Own:

Both the poet and the father speak eloquently in this letter of William Carlos Williams. It is a characteristic piece from a writer who has been called outspoken, goodhearted and generous. "Williams"—Randall Jarrell has written—"loves, blames, and yells despairingly at the Little Men just as naturally and legitimately as Saint-Loup got angry at the servants: because he *feels,* not just says, that the differences between men are less important than their similarities—that he and you and I, together, are the Little Men." What Williams felt about his son, and the job of molding a life, is clear enough.

March 13, 1935

Dearest Bill: This I can say for certain, you seem not far different from what I was myself at your age. I don't mind saying I went through hell . . . what with worrying about my immortal soul and my hellish itch to screw almost any female I could get my hands on—which I never did. I can tell you it is almost as vivid today as it was then when I hear you speak of it. Everything seems upside down and one's self the very muck under one's foot.

It comes from many things, my dear boy, but mostly from the inevitable maladjustment consequent upon growing up in a more or less civilized environment. . . . But more immediately, your difficulties arise from a lack of balance in your daily life, a lack of balance which has to be understood and withstood—for it cannot be avoided for the present. I refer to the fact that your

142

intellectual life, for the moment, has eclipsed the physical life, the animal life, the normal he-man life, which every man needs and craves. If you were an athlete, a powerful body, one who could be a hero on the field or the diamond, a *Big Hero,* many of your mental tortures would be lulled to sleep. But you cannot be that—so what? You'll have to wait and take it by a different course.

You, dear Bill, have a magnificent opportunity to enjoy life ahead of you. You have sensibility (even if it drives you nuts at times) which will be the source of keen pleasures later and the source of useful accomplishments too. You've got a brain, as you have been told *ad nauseum.* But these are things which are tormenting you, the very things which are your most valuable possessions and which will be your joy tomorrow. Sure you are sentimental, sure you admire a man like Wordsworth and his "Tintern Abbey." It is natural, it is the correct reaction of your age to life. It is also a criticism of Wordsworth as you will see later. All I can say about that is, wait! Not wait cynically, idly, but wait while looking, believing, getting fooled, changing from day to day. Wait with the only kind of faith I have ever recognized, the faith that says I wanna know! I wanna see! I think I will understand when I do know and see. Meanwhile I'm not making any final judgments. Wait it out. Don't worry too much. You've got time. You're all right. You're reacting to life in the only way an intelligent, sensitive young man in college can. In another year you'll enter another sphere of existence, the practical one. The knowledge, abstract now, which seems unrelated to sense to you (at times) will get a different color. . . .

Mother and I both send love. Don't let *anything* get your goat and don't think you have to duck anything in life. There is a way out for every man who has the intellectual fortitude to go on in the face of difficulties.

Yours,
Dad

Once, in a short poem, Williams asked, "Are not my children as dear to me as falling leaves. . . ?"

✳   ✳   ✳

"*. . . it's better to call older men Mister.*"

Ogden Nash Reacts to an Affair
of a Foolish Heart:

After finishing school, Isabel Nash persuaded her parents to let her go abroad for a year. "While I was visiting some family friends in Paris," she wrote later, "I met an 'older man' who flattered me immensely. He sought me out, talked to me, and expressed what I thought were the most fascinating and sophisticated views on life. One day he told me that he and his wife, from whom he had long been separated, were getting a divorce. The romantic alchemy that affects some silly girls convinced me that he was madly in love with me." Isabel wrote first an ecstatic letter, then spent a night considering the proposal, and wrote again to her family—the second time more reassuringly. Her father's response to the two letters follows:

Dearest Isabel,

I gather that by now you have decided Mr. X is too old for you, as well as being a very silly man, but I am not pleased

144

by the episode and I trust that by now you aren't either. The propensity of old men for flirting with young girls has been the object of coarse merriment since primeval days, as I should think your reading, if nothing else, should have told you.

You should be intelligent enough to know that in various eras of history it has been fashionable to laugh at morals, but the fact of the matter is that Old Man Morals just keeps rolling along and the laughers end up as driftwood on a sandbar. You can't beat the game, because morals as we know them represent the sum of the experience of the race. That is why it distressed me to find you glibly tossing off references to divorce. You surely have seen enough of its effects on your friends to know that it is a tragic thing even when forced on one partner by the vices of the other.

Read the marriage vows again—they are not just words, not even just a poetic promise to God. They are a practical promise to yourself to be happy. This I know from simply looking around me.

It bothers me to think that you may have sloppy—not sophisticated but sloppy—ideas about life. I have never tried to blind you to any side of life, through any form of censorship, trusting in your intelligence to learn of, and to recognize, evil without approving or participating in it. So please throw Iris March and all the golden doomed Bohemian girls away and be Isabel—there's more fun in it for you.

Keep on having your gay time, but just keep yourself in hand, and remember that generally speaking it's better to call older men Mister.

> I love you tremendously,
> Daddy

The trust and faith of her parents, Miss Nash wrote, "was somehow much more binding than the most stringent rules laid down by many other parents. I know that I've never been unhappier than when, after this silly flirtation, I felt I had fallen in Daddy's estimation."

*   *   *

'Well, my boy, I think that is better than being king."

Damon Runyon Writes a Temperance Letter and a Word About His Life:

Damon Runyon, Jr., has in a fine book told of his relationship with his father and of his own fight against alcoholism. Father and son had been at odds for many years after Damon Runyon's divorce from his first wife. Damon, Jr., had followed his father into the newspaper business and had discovered the burden of carrying a famous name. Succumbing to the comfort he found in liquor, he lost one job after another until, at twenty-six, he joined Alcoholics Anonymous, and later reported this fact to his father. "I told him I didn't know what his reactions would be to virtual public admission of my plight, but that I was convinced it was my only hope for tomorrow and I was going to stick to it regardless of what he thought. . . . My report brought a quick reply from my father with the story of his own battle with the bottle."

July 3, 1945

My Dear Son:

I was delighted to hear from you and greatly relieved as I did not know just where you were or what you were doing.

To say that I am pleased with your good report is putting it very mildly. It is the best news I have heard in a long time.

I think the samples of your work that you sent are excellent reporting with a swell human interest touch. I have always thought you could write and it has always been my hope that you would carry on what I think is an honorable name in the newspaper game, the greatest profession in the world.

You will improve the more you write. Good writing is simply a matter of application but I learned many years ago that words will not put themselves down on paper in dreams or in conversations.

You have been on my mind a great deal lately. Mary [Runyon's daughter] and I were having dinner at Lindy's one night recently and I wrote her a note (my only means of communication with people now) saying I wondered where you were.

"I have been thinking of him all day," she said. "It's his birthday."

She was as pleased as I with your letter. . . .

I know more about Alcoholics Anonymous than you might think. I read a great deal about the organization and I had several contacts with active participants on the Pacific Coast. One worked at Fox when I was making *Irish Eyes Are Smiling*.

I think it may be one of the great movements of all time and I am extremely pleased that it has aroused your interest.

Surely by this time you must have learned that you were not cut out for a drinking man. Drinking is not hereditary as some rumpots like to alibi, but I think there are certain strains that are alergic to alcohol and you seem to carry that strain.

You ask me about my own experiences. I quit drinking thirty-five years ago in Denver and have not had a drink since.

I quit because I realized that I got no fun out of drinking. Liquor only gave me delusions of grandeur that got me into trouble. It never made me happy and bright and sparkling as it does some people. It made me dull and stupid and quarrelsome. It made me dreadfully ill afterwards. I did not have the constitution to drink. It rendered me helpless. It destroyed my pride, my sense of decency.

I quit because I saw that I was not going to get anywhere in the world if I didn't, and I wanted to go places. I was sorely tempted many times, usually in moments of elation over some small triumph or when I was feeling sorry for myself, a strong characteristic of the drinker, but I managed to stand it off.

It was never taking that first drink that saved me.

I had to endure loneliness and even derision as a result of my abstinence for some years but it eventually became a matter of such general knowledge that no one pressed me to take a drink any more and finally I became positively famous for hanging out with drunks and never touching a drop.

We could have saved many a great career with an organization like the A.A.'s in the old days when a lush was shunned even more than he is today.

You stick to your organization and try to help other fellows unfortunate enough to be under the spell of old John Barleycorn. No good ever comes of drinking and I don't think any bad ever comes of *not* drinking.

So much for my temperance lecture, except that I have only a little time left as you may surmise from my ailment, but I will go happy if I know that you have conquered your enemy. If you have gone eight months without drinking, you would be a fool to ever start again, knowing what you know.

I will be sixty-five in October. I get around all right and

feel pretty well but I live under a shadow. I have to see the doctor every week. I do my daily column and a Sunday feature and last month I wrote two fiction stories for *Collier's*.

I have to keep plugging away at an age when I thought I would be in retirement, because my illness practically broke me. I went to Hollywood at a salary of over $2,000 a week largely as a matter of satisfying my vanity—I thought it was wonderful to be able to command that kind of income at sixty-three—forgetting that it only added to my normal income and increased my taxes.

Well, the upshot was the government taxes took most of it, and when I became ill and the big money was shut off entirely the doctors and the hospitals cut up what was left. I am now living not only on borrowed time but practically on borrowed money. But having seen others similarly afflicted I know that I have no kick coming.

Your A.A.'s should give you something you never had—sympathy for your fellow man. It was not your fault that you didn't have it. It was just the way you were gaited.

That is one element a writer must have to be a good writer —sympathy. What we call "Heart" . . .

I will not again write to you at this length. But I am so glad to hear that you are getting along all right I am a little windier than usual.

I am quite pleased that we are in opposing papers. I have been in the *Enquirer* off and on for years—usually off. You are with a fine outfit, the Scripps-Howard. I think it is better for a young writer than any other. The kind of work you are doing is exactly the kind you need because it gives you human contact and a knowledge of how people live.

You say that you don't know if you will ever be anything

more than a better than average reporter. Well, my boy, I think that is better than being king. I do indeed.

Mary sends her love and I sign myself in deepest affection.

Dad

*　　*　　*

"You have only one friend, my son,
and that is your courage."

Dagobert Runes Points Out to a Son the Problems of Being a Jew:

Editor, teacher of philosophy and biographer of Goethe, Dagobert D. Runes is a writer who has dealt with many facets of the Hebrew impact on the civilization of the Western World. Below is one of his letters to his growing son in which he deals bluntly with some of the problems inherent in prejudice.

[1948]

My Little Man,

As you know, I have never addressed you as "my little child" the way people are accustomed to address children. They like to create two worlds, the world of the child and the world of the man. In the world of the child virtue seems to abound, justice to flower, and kindness and tolerance to flourish. Ah, but in the world of man the ways are crooked, the designs are evil, and the interests malicious. And so they let you live your early

150

years in the childhood world of make believe only to awaken you when maturity takes you into the reality of a most sorrowful existence. And while you still rub your eyes—were you dreaming? were you seeing things?—all the pretty, warm and playful children grow into mean, designing, envious men and women.

It was all right for you, my little man, to play with a colored girl with marbles and hoop and swing; but now if you were only to walk down the street with her hand-in-hand, they would point their fingers at you and cast you from their group like a leper.

It was all right for you, my son, to share your cot with the German lad; but now the school which he enters is closed to you and you must hunt for your learning until you find a back bench that they have put aside for you perhaps a thousand miles away.

That is why I never called you "child," my little man. I didn't want you to rise too high in the skyward climb of early dreams, only to fall on the rocky face of this infested globe.

Remember when I took you to that little town in Georgia and seated you in a classroom and you listened to a wise old teacher talk about American democracy and freedom for all and the pursuit of happiness, and how I suddenly poked you in the ribs and you began to cry and asked me why? I told you, "Don't be a dreamy fool. Just wait." And I took you across the street into the park and showed you the public fountain. Upon the stony base was engraved, "For whites only." And I told you of another park in another country where the schools were even bigger than in Georgia and the churches more cathedral. There was a beautiful sandy beach, but in the center a huge placard said, "Jews Keep Out."

That fountain-base in Georgia, that placard in Germany,

were not put up by evil-minded persons who live on the fringe of the community. These ugly deeds were perpetrated by the people in authority, by the very same people who teach their children democracy and preach the good Christian life to them in their churches.

They have made a mint of words, these people, but these words are not coins any longer. They are chips. There is neither gold in them nor silver, only some worthless plastic which they pass to each other in secret and open gentlemen's agreements—and just try to cash these chips. Let a Negro man try to ask for full value at work or at play or even at prayer. The very man who preaches that all men are God's children, equal before Him and the Holy Ghost and the loving Christ, would turn him out of the church.

If you are a Hebrew there are a thousand schools that will not accept you, a thousand homes that will not house you, a thousand bosses who will not hire you.

Democracy, equality, dignity—these are chips, my son, not coins. They may be cashed only by members, and never forget that although you and your black brother may often be guests, you can never be members. It is odd that some of these chips should bear the likeness of Christ—*Love Thy Neighbor* is the engraved motto. Others bear the motto of Moses: the *Ten Commandments* are on the reverse side. Both were Israelites; one even an African born on the Nile. Perhaps these coins were cut only in irony—how little do these people love their Israelite neighbors, and have the Commandments ever been applied to the Africans?

Since you were knee-high, my son, I have taught you the worthlessness of these coins. Six millions of your brothers and sisters were poisoned and burned, hunted, tortured, drowned and

152

bludgeoned, butchered and choked, garroted and guillotined, denounced and strung up by seventy million well-educated Christians living in the heart of Europe. And the world of Christian men went about its business, deaf to the cries of mothers who saw their children cut up before their eyes, of children who were made to watch the agonies of their choking parents. You see, even then, in the face of these most devilish of abominations, the people of the Christian world were not concerned with the fate of your victimized brothers and sisters. They would rather forgive the skinning alive of your brothers than forget your own slightest transgression.

There are no children among the beleaguered, my son. We Israelites live on a rock surrounded by an ocean of hate, suspicion, and indifference, and we may never know when and where the next storm may come. You must be alert, my son, alert and fighting-ready. You can never really be a child in such turmoil. Never fear so long as you stand on the rock of Israel's heritage and so long as you do not let them set you to dreaming with their sirenic fables and promises. You have only one friend, my son, and that is your courage. And like that mythological figure of old, when you leave the rock of your heritage, gone is your strength and your future. Be strong, my son.

Your loving
Father

IV

* * *

Heritage and
the Helping Hand

*. . . the recognition of one's
own roots . . . and the guiding touch
of experience . . .*

Lorenzo the Magnificent to His Son,
the Future Pope:

Lorenzo de' Medici has been described as a man of scandalous immorality. Though Florence was nominally a republic, this Medici was lord of all, and virtually a tyrant. He kept an army of spies, intervened in his people's most private affairs and exalted men of the lowest order to positions of great authority. On the friendliest terms with Pope Innocent VIII, Lorenzo, in the spring of 1492, obtained the exaltation of his sixteen-year-old son Giovanni to the college of cardinals. Sick—perhaps knowing that he was on his deathbed—the father sought to guide his son, who had not become a priest, in the very ways that Lorenzo had done his pagan best to ignore throughout his life.

[April, 1492]

You, and all of us who are interested in your welfare, ought to esteem ourselves highly favored by Providence, not only for the many honors and benefits bestowed on our house, but more particularly for having conferred upon us, in your person, the greatest dignity we have ever enjoyed. This favor, in itself so important, is rendered still more so by the circumstances with which it is accompanied, and especially by the consideration of your youth and of our situation in the world.

The first thing that I would therefore suggest to you is that you ought to be grateful to God, and continually to recollect that it is not through your merits, your prudence, or your solicitude, that this event has taken place, but through his favor, which you can only repay by a pious, chaste, and exemplary life; and that your obligations to the performance of these duties are so much the greater, as in your early years you have given some reasonable expectation that your riper age may produce such fruits. It would indeed be highly disgraceful, and as contrary to your duty as to my hopes, if, at a time when others display a greater share of reason and adopt a better mode of life, you should forget the precepts of your youth, and forsake the path in which you have hitherto trodden.

Endeavor therefore to alleviate the burthen of your early dignity by the regularity of your life and by your perseverence in those studies which are suitable to your profession. It gave me great satisfaction to learn that, in the course of the past year, you had frequently, on your own accord, gone to communion and confession; nor do I conceive that there is any better way of obtaining the favor of heaven than by habituating yourself to a performance of these and similar duties. This appears to me to be the most suitable and useful advice which, in the first instance, I can possibly give you.

I well know that as you are now to reside at Rome, that sink of all iniquity, the difficulty of conducting yourself by these admonitions will be increased. The influence of example is itself prevalent; but you will probably meet with those who will particularly endeavor to corrupt and incite you to vice; because, as you may yourself perceive, your early attainment to so great a dignity is not observed without envy, and those who could not prevent your receiving that honor will secretly endeavor to diminish it, by inducing you to forfeit the good estimation of the public: thereby precipitating you into that gulf into which they had fallen themselves; in which attempt, the consideration of your youth will give them a confidence and success.

To these difficulties you ought to oppose yourself with the greater firmness, as there is at present less virtue amongst your brethren of the college. I acknowledge indeed that several of them are good and learned men, whose lives are exemplary, and whom I would recommend to you as patterns for your conduct. By emulating them you will be so much the more known and esteemed, in proportion as your age and the peculiarity of your situation will distinguish you from your colleagues. Avoid, however, as you would Scylla or Charybdis, the imputation of hypocrisy; guard against all ostentation, either in your conduct or your discourse; affect not austerity, nor even appear too serious. This advice you will, I hope, in time understand and practice better than I can express it.

Yet you are not unacquainted with the great importance of the character which you have to sustain, for you well know that all the Christian world would prosper if the cardinals were what they ought to be; because in such a case there would always be a good Pope, upon which the tranquility of Christendom so materially depends. Endeavor then to render yourself such, that if all the rest resembled you, we might expect this universal blessing. To give you particular directions as to your behavior and conversation would be a matter of no small difficulty. I shall therefore only recommend that in your intercourse with the cardinals and other men of rank, your language be unassuming and respectful, guiding yourself, however, by your own reason, and not submitting to be impelled by the passions of others, who actuated by improper motives, may pervert the use of their reason. Let it satisfy your conscience that your conversation is without intentional offense; and if, through impetuosity of temper, anyone should be offended, as his enmity is without just cause, so it will not be very lasting. On this, your first visit to Rome, it will however be more adviseable for you to listen to others than to speak much yourself.

You are now devoted to God and the church; on which account you ought to aim at being a good ecclesiastic, and to show that you prefer the honor and the state of the church and of the apostolic see to every other consideration. Nor, while you keep this in view, will it be difficult for you to favor your family and your native place. On the contrary, you should be the link to bind this city closer to the church, and our family with the city; and although it be impossible to foresee what accidents may happen, yet I doubt not but this may be done with equal advantage to all; observing, however, that you are always to prefer the interests of the church.

You are not only the youngest cardinal in the college, but the youngest person that ever was raised to that rank; and you ought therefore to be the most vigilant and unassuming, not giving others occasion to wait for you, either in the chapel, the consistory, or upon deputations. You will soon get sufficient insight into the manners of your brethren. With those of less respectable character converse not with too much intimacy; not merely on account of the circumstance itself, but for the sake of public opinion. Converse on general topics with all. On public occasions let your equipage and dress be rather below than above mediocrity. A handsome house and a well-ordered family will be preferable to a great retinue and a splendid residence. Endeavor to live with regularity, and gradually to bring your expenses within those bonds which in a new establishment cannot perhaps be expected. Silk and jewels are not suitable for persons in your station. Your taste will be better shown in the acquisition of a few elegant remains of antiquity, or in the collecting of handsome books, and by your attendants being learned and well bred rather than numerous. Invite others to your house oftener than you receive invitations. Practice neither too frequently.

Let your own food be plain, and take sufficient exercise, for those who wear your habit are soon liable, without great caution, to contract infirmities. The station of a cardinal is not less secure than elevated; on which account those who arrive at it too frequently become negligent, conceiving that their object is attained, and that they can preserve it with little trouble. This idea is often injurious to the life and character of those who entertain it. Be attentive therefore to your conduct, and confide in others too little rather than too much.

There is one rule which I would recommend to your attention in preference to all others: rise early in the morning. This will not only contribute to your health, but will enable you to arrange and expedite the business of the day; and as there are various duties incident to your station, such as the performance of divine services, studying, giving audience, &c., you will find the observance of this admonition productive of the greatest utility.

Another very necessary precaution, particularly on your entrance into public life, is to deliberate every morning on what you may have to perform the following day, that you may not be unprepared for whatever may happen. With respect to your speaking in the consistory, it will be most becoming for you at present to refer the matters in debate to the judgment of His Holiness, alleging as a reason your own youth and inexperience. You will probably be desired to intercede for the favors of the Pope on particular occasions. Be cautious, however, that you trouble him not too often; for his temper leads him to be most liberal to those who weary him least with their solicitations. This you must observe, lest you should give him offense, remember-

ing also at times to converse with him on more agreeable topics;
and if you should be obliged to request some kindness from him,
let it be done with that modesty and humility which are so pleasing to his disposition. Farewell.

Lorenzo soon died. Two years later, the young cardinal was
expelled along with the rest of the Medici when Charles VIII
invaded Florence. For a while Giovanni dallied on the Continent,
then tried unsuccessfully to recapture Florence. Finally, when
Pope Julius II died in 1513, Cardinal Medici was elected pope
at the age of thirty-eight—in a single week being ordained to
the priesthood, consecrated as bishop and enthroned with the
name Leo X. He is reported to have said that God gave the
papacy to the Medici for their delight. His father's deathbed
advice was well forgotten.

*   *   *

*"I wish you would draw
one bird only, on a twig . . ."*

Audubon Instructs a Son Who Is About to Become His Assistant:

John James Audubon, who himself had begun to draw birds as
a boy, made his two sons his assistants when they were still
in their teens. He had by then abandoned his various attempts
at a career in business, and with the support of his wife had
collected and painted the first of his *Birds in America*. With
this material he went to England in 1826 to find a publisher,
and his genius was immediately recognized by scientific and

art circles. For the next dozen years he divided his time between Europe and the United States, and in 1827 he wrote the letters below to his fifteen-year-old son, John Woodhouse Audubon.

My dear John—

I am thankfull to you for your letters continue to write from time to time, draw, and study music closely, there is time for all things—I give you my Gun with all my Heart best wishes, but earn it at your Dear Mamma's will—God bless You——

Your Father and Friend
John J. Audubon

This hint of the youngster's interest in drawing came out in the open in Audubon's letter to John, written in August of the same year:

I would give you 500 dollars per annum were you able to make for me such drawings as I will want. I wish you would draw one bird only, on a twig, and send it [to me] to look at, as soon as you can after reciving this letter. . . . I should like to have a large box filled with branches of the trees, covered with mosses &c., such as Mamma knows I want; now recollect, all sorts of Birds, males and females, ugly or handsome.

John Woodhouse Audubon and his brother Victor worked side by side with their father until his death in 1851; together they finished Audubon's *The Viviparous Quadrupeds of North America,* of which the younger John painted nearly half of the illustrations.

＊   ＊   ＊

163

Mendelssohn's Father Gives Some Opinions of a Musical Amateur:

Abraham Mendelssohn used to describe himself as "the son of my father and the father of my son." He was indeed the son of Moses Mendelssohn, the great Jewish philosopher, and the parent of Felix Mendelssohn-Bartholdy. Yet, though he had no musical talent, he had enormous influence on his son's genius. It was he who was selected Mendelssohn's teachers and tutors, who supervised his studies and created a home atmosphere in which the precocious child grew up naturally, despite the strain of continuous public appearances. He could also put his finger on a deficiency in his son's composition of *Ave Maria:*

Berlin, March 10, 1835

This is the third letter I have written you this week, and if it goes, reading my letters will become a permanent item in the distribution of your time budget; but you must blame yourself for this, as you will spoil me by your praise.

I will pass at once to the musical portion of your last letter. Your aphorism, that every room in which Sebastian Bach is sung is transformed into a church, I consider particularly appropriate; and when I once heard the last movement of the piece in question, it made a similar impression on me, otherwise I confess that I cannot overcome my dislike for figured chorales in general, because I cannot understand the fundamental idea on which they are based, especially where the contending voices maintain constant balance of power. For example, in the first chorus of the "Passion"—where the chorale forms only a more important and consistent part of the basis; or where, as in the above mentioned movement of the cantata (if I remember it rightly, hav-

ing only heard it once) the chorale represents the principal building, and the individual parts only the ornaments—I can better
figure the purpose and the conception, but definitely not where
the passage in a particular manner carries out variations on the
theme. Assuredly no liberties should ever be taken with a chorale.
Its highest purpose is that the congregation should sing it in all
its purity to the accompaniment of the organ; all else seems to
me idle and inappropriate for a church.

At Fanny's last morning's musical the motet of Bach, "Got-
tes Zeit is die allerbeste Zeit", and your "Ave Maria" were
sung by selected voices. A long passage in the middle of the latter, as well as the end, appeared to me too learned and intricate
to accord with the simple and pious, although certainly genuine
Catholic spirit, which pervades the music. Rebecca's remark that
there was some confusion in the execution of those very passages
which I considered too intricate only proves that I am an ignor-
amus, but not that the end is not too abstrusely modulated. . . .
Your intention to restore Händel to his original form has led me
to some reflections on his later style of instrumentation. A question is not unfrequently raised as to whether Händel, if he had
written in our day, would have made use of all the existing musical facilities in composing his oratorios—which in fact only
means: would the wonted artistic form to which we give the
name of Händel assume the same shape now that it did a hundred years ago; and the answer to this presents itself at once.
The question, however, ought to be put in a different form; not
whether Händel would have composed his oratorios now as he
did a century ago, but, rather, whether he would have composed
oratorios at all. Hardly—if they had to be written in the style of
those of today.

From my saying this to you, you may gather with what

eager anticipation and confidence I look forward to your own oratorio, which will, I trust, solve the problem of combining ancient conceptions with modern means. Otherwise the result would be as great a failure as that of the painters of the nineteenth century, who only make themselves ridiculous by attempting to revive the religious content of the fifteenth, with its long arms and legs and topsy-turvy perspective. These new resources seem to me, like everything else in the world, to have been developed just at the right time for animating the inner impulses which were daily becoming more feeble. The heights of religious feeling on which Bach, Händel, and their contemporaries stood, were such that they required no large orchestras for their oratorios; and I well remember from my earliest years that the "Messiah", "Judas" and "Alexander's Feast", were given exactly as Händel wrote them, without even an organ, and yet to the delight and edification of everyone.

But how is this matter to be stopped nowadays, when vacuity of thought and noise in music are gradually being developed in inverse ratio to each other? The orchestra is now established and is likely to maintain its present form without any essential modification, for a long time to come. Wealth is a fault only when we do not know how to use it. How, then, is the wealth of the orchestra to be applied? What guidance can the poet give for this, and in what regions? Or is music to be entirely severed from poetry, and work its own independent way? I do not believe it can accomplish the latter; at least, only to a very limited extent, and—in general—not authentically. To effect the former, an object must be found for music—just as for painting—which by its fervor, its universal sufficiency and perspicuity may take the place of the pious emotion of former days. It seems to me that also from this point of view both the oratorios of Haydn are remarkable phenomena. The poems of both, as poems, are weak, but they have happily substituted the old positive and almost metaphysical religious impulses with those which nature, as a visible emanation of the Godhead, in her universality and her thousandfold individualities, instils in every susceptible heart. Hence the profound depth, but also the cheerful efficiency, and certainly genuine religious influence of these two works, which hitherto stand by themselves. Hence the combined effect of the playful and detached passages with the most noble and sincere feelings of gratitude produced by the whole; hence it is, also, that I, individually, would like as little to be deprived—in the "Creation" and in "The Seasons"—of the crowing of the cock, the singing of the lark, the lowing of the cattle, and the rustic glee of the peasants, as in nature herself. In other words, the "Creation" and "The Seasons" are founded on nature and on the visible service of God; and are no new materials for music to be found there?

The publication of "Goethe's Correspondence with a Child" I consider a most provoking and pernicious abuse of the press, through which, more and more rapidly, all illusions will be destroyed, without which life is only death. You, I trust, will never lose your illusions, and ever preserve your filial attachment to your father.

In response, the twenty-six-year-old composer struck to the heart of Abraham Mendelssohn's peroration. "I often cannot understand," Felix wrote, "how it is possible to have so acute a judgment as regards music, without being yourself technically musical; and if I could express what I assuredly feel, with as much clearness and intuitive perception as you do, as soon as you enter upon the subject, I never would make another obscure speech all my life long. I thank you a thousand times for this. . . . I ought to feel rather provoked that you discovered after only one imperfect hearing of my composition what I found out after long familiarity; but, again, it makes me happy that you have such a definite sense of music; for the deficiencies in the middle movement and at the end consist of such minute faults —which might have been remedied by a very few notes, mainly cancellations—that neither I nor any other musician would have been aware of them without hearing the piece repeatedly because as a rule we seek the cause much deeper. . . ."

✳   ✳   ✳

". . . I am the sensation of
Europe and America . . ."

Heinrich Schliemann Spurs His Son to Emulate Himself:

"Now comes a fairy tale," says C. W. Ceram in *Gods, Graves and Scholars*, "the story of the poor boy who at the age of seven dreamed of finding a city, and who thirty-nine years later went forth, sought, and found not only the city but also treasure such as the world had not seen since the loot of the conquistadors." Left behind when Heinrich Schliemann started his search for Troy were a wife, who refused to share his passion for archaeology, and a teenage son to whom he wrote words of glowing self-congratulation that seldom, surely, have been surpassed.

[Paris, June 24, 1870]

To Serge Schliemann

I have received your good letters of May 24 and June 4, and am sad to learn that you aren't advancing. In this life one

168

must progress continually if one isn't to become discouraged. Try to follow the example of your father who—in whatever situation—always proved what a man can accomplish by sheer energy. During the four years in Amsterdam, from 1842 to 1846, I truly performed wonders. I did what never has been done before, nor ever will be done again. Later when I was in business in St. Petersburg, I was the most successful and at the same time the most prudent dealer on the stock exchange. When I began to travel, I was a traveler par excellence. No St. Petersburg merchant has ever written a learned book, but I have written one that has been translated into four languages, and is universally admired. At the moment, as an archaeologist, I am the sensation of Europe and America because I have discovered the ancient city of Troy, that Troy for which archaeologists of the entire world have searched in vain for the past two thousand years. . . .

Troy was not enough. Schliemann was in love with Greece, and he chose an Athenian as his second wife, "a girl as beautiful as the pyramids" who shared his passion for archaeology. Together they dug to their heart's content, and discovered the royal tombs of Mycenae, the treasury of Minyas, and the grandeur of the Tiryns palace—Schliemann's first family was lost in the wake of these successes.

* * *

Henry James Is Offered a Helping Hand
by Henry James, Sr.:

The James family was as closely knit as any in history—not only because of their intellect, but because of their emotional need for each other. Henry James, Sr., a millionaire son of an Irish immigrant who was brought up in Albany, New York, used his wealth to further his interest in religio-philosophy and to encourage his children's careers [p. 22]. When Henry James began to write, the senior James led family forums in which the tyro's work was neatly dissected, frequently with profit. But the father was not as successful in telling his son *what* to write; this letter was written in 1873 to his "darling Harry" when the latter was in Rome.

[Cambridge, Massachusetts]

I went to see Osgood about publishing a selection of your Tales. He repeated what he told you: that he would give you fifteen per cent, do all the advertising etc., you paying for the plates: or he would pay everything and give you *ten* per cent on every copy sold after the first thousand. I shall be willing (in case you would like to publish, and I think it is time for you to do so) to bear the expense of stereotyping, and if you will pick out what you would like to be included, we shall set to work at once, and have the book ready by next autumn. I have got the materials of a story for you which I was telling Willy of the other day as a regular Tourgenieff subject, and he told me to send it off to you at once, he was so struck with it. Matthew Henry Webster was a very cultivated and accomplished young man in Albany, at the time I was growing up. He belonged to a respectable family, (of booksellers and publishers) was himself bred to the law, but had such a love of literature and, especially, of the natural sciences, that he never devoted himself very strictly to his profession. He was the intimate friend of Professor Henry and other distinguished men of science, corresponded with foreign scientific bodies, and his contributions to science were of so original a cast as to suggest great hopes of his future eminence. He *was a polished gentleman, of perfect address, brave as Caesar, utterly unegotistic,* and one's wonder was how he ever grew up in Albany or reconciled himself to living in the place. One day he invested some money in a scheme much favoured by the President of the Bank in which he deposited, and his adventure proved a fortune.

There lived also a family in Albany of the name of Kane (Mary Port's step-mother being of its members) and this family reckoned upon a great social sensation in bringing out their youngest daughter, (Lydia Sybil Kane) who had never been seen by mortal eye outside her own family, except that of a physician, who reported that she was fabulously beautiful. She *was* the most beautiful girl I think I ever saw, at a little distance. Well, she made her sensation, and brought Mr. Webster incontinently to her feet. Her family wanted wealth above all things for her; but here was wealth and something more, very much more, and they smiled upon his suit. Everything went merrily for a while. Webster was profoundly intoxicated with his prize. Never was man so enamoured, and never was beauty better fitted to receive adoration. She was of an exquisite Grecian outline as to face, with a countenance like the tender dawn, and form and manners ravishingly graceful. But Webster was not content with his adventure—embarked again and lost all he owned almost. Mr. Oliver Kane (or Mrs., for she was the ruler of the family and as hard as the nether world in heart) gave the cue to her daughter, and my friend was dismissed. He couldn't believe his senses. He raved and cursed his fate. But it was inexorable. What was to be done? With a bitterness of heart inconceivable he plucked his revenge by marrying instantly a stout and blooming jade who in respect to Miss Kane was as a peony to a violet, and who was absolutely nothing but flesh and blood. Her he bore upon his arm at fashionable hours through the streets; her he took to church, preserving his exquisite ease and courtesy to everyone, as if absolutely nothing had occurred; and her he pretended to take to his bosom in private, with what a shudder one can imagine. Everybody stood aghast. He went daily about his affairs, as serene and unconscious as the moon in the heavens. Soon his poverty showed itself in certain economies of his wardrobe which had always been very recherché. Soon again he broke his leg, and went about on crutches, but neither poverty nor accident had the *least* power to ruffle his perfect repose. He was always superior to his circumstances, met you exactly as he had always done, impressed you invariably as the best bred man you ever saw, and left you wondering what a heart and what a brain lay behind such a fortune.

One morning we all read in the paper at breakfast that Mr. Henry Webster had appealed the day before to the protection of the police against his wife, who had beaten him, and whom as a woman he could not degrade by striking in return; and the police responded promptly to his appeal. He went about his affairs as usual that day and every day, never saying a word to any one of his trouble, nor even indirectly asking sympathy, but compelling you to feel that here if anywhere was a novel height of manhood, a self-respect so eminent as to look down with scorn upon every refuge open to ordinary human infirmity. This lasted five or six years. He never drank, had no vice, in fact of any kind, and lived a life of such decorum, so far as his own action was concerned, a life of such interest in science and literature as to be the most delightful and unconscious of companions even when his coat was shabby beyond compare, and you dare not look at him for fear of betraying your own vulgar misintelligence.

Finally Sybil Kane died smitten with small pox, and all her beauty gone to hideousness. He lingered awhile, his beautiful manners undismayed still, his eye as undaunted as at the beginning, and then suddenly died. I never knew his equal in manhood, sheer, thorough, manly force, competent to itself in every emergency, and seeking none of the ordinary subterfuges which men seek in order to hide their own imbecility. I think it is a good basis for a novel.

Henry James sent his thanks to his father in a letter to his mother: "It is admirable material . . . I have transcribed it in my notebook with religious care, and think that some day something will come of it." But forty years later he put it this way: "As for the recital, in such detail, of the theme of a possible literary effort . . . how could I feel this, when it reached me, as anything but a sign of the admirable anxiety with which thought could be taken, even though 'amateurishly,' in my professional interest?—since professional I by that time appeared able to pass for being."

* * *

A Shakespearean Scholar Points to the Artistry of Charlotte Brontë:

Although a member of the bar, Horace Howard Furness devoted his life to the study of Shakespeare and, in 1871, brought out the first volume of a Variorum edition of the plays designed to represent and illustrate the conclusions of the best scholars in all languages. It has been said that "few have so brightened erudition with unvarying gentleness, sanity and humor." Furness's sharp insights were not confined to Shakespeare—as is witnessed by the letter below to his son and namesake.

222 Washington Square
17 Nov., '86

Dearest Horrie

. . . Into this world of sawdust dolls with simpering faces Charlotte Brontë dashed a brilliant headstrong girl, plain as a pikestaff, but with every intellectual quality that can fascinate a man—and after making her marry a crippled, scarred, burnt, blind man set the world screaming itself hoarse with applause. It is an epoch-making book, my boy. The world of novels has never seen such a revulsion: and its effects have lasted to this hour. Let any writer attempt to give us another Laura Matilda of the ante Jane Eyre type and vouz markez mes mots there'll be a tee-hee. No, no, dear boy, read Jane Eyre historically, note the artistic design of the authoress, and then you'll see clear enough why she made her heroine ugly. Had Jane Eyre been pretty you'd never have read the story—it wouldn't have survived a month.

174

Dearest love to Will—

Your old most loving
Father

The son to whom this letter is addressed became a partner and successor to his father's work, issuing the last of the fifteen volumes of the Variorum edition of Shakespeare in 1913. In 1922, he edited his father's letters.

*　　*　　*

". . . the strength of incontestable,
if not uncontested, talent."

Camille Pissarro Encourages a Painter Son:

At the time this letter was written, Pissarro was experimenting with the pointillist method of crowding a canvas with small spots of color. His son, Lucien, was in London, beginning his own painting career.

Eragny [May 15, 1888]

My dear Lucien,

I think you would do well to come here, for if you wait indefinitely for your money you will miss the good weather; come now while we have some money and prepare for your exhibition for next year and also do some illustrations. It is necessary not to be discouraged; one must get oneself accepted on the strength of incontestable, if not uncontested, talent. Renouard made his name on the strength of three or four illustrations of scenes backstage and lady painters in the Louvre, while these are far from being comparable to the works of Degas they were quite good, they lacked style but there was energy, they were not the works of a nonentity, and Renouard made his mark. I believe myself when one has talent one finally breaks through; thus when the occasion presents itself for working freely do not miss it.

I work a great deal in the studio; the leaves are burgeoning and don't give me a chance to work out a single sketch. I am making little water colors and pastels, I believe that it doesn't go too badly; in the studio I am preparing five or six canvases, I work on one after another, I'm getting used to working so.

Lucien Pissarro never achieved greatness, and his father abandoned pointillism to return to a broader manner—in his last years producing some of his finest paintings. Arnold Hauser, in his *Social History of Art,* has underscored the economic plight that this father and son shared: "The impressionists certainly did not make it easy for people to understand their artistic ideas —but in what a bad way the art appreciation of the public must have been to allow such great, honest and peaceable artists as Monet, Renoir and Pissarro almost to starve."

*　　*　　*

*"A masterpiece could be made
of a dish of turnips."*

Sherwood Anderson Compares the Arts of Writing and Painting:

In the winter of 1926–27 Sherwood Anderson had been in Paris
with his daughter Marion and his son John, a young painter.
"Sherwood Anderson does dress well and his son John follows
suit," Gertrude Stein wrote of their visit in *The Autobiography
of Alice B. Toklas.* "While Sherwood was still in Paris John the
son was an awkward shy boy. The day after Sherwood left John
turned up, sat easily on the arm of the sofa and was beautiful to
look upon and he knew it. Nothing to the outward eye had
changed but he had changed and he knew it." John may have been
glad to be in Paris without his father's watchful eye, but he continued to turn to his parent for advice on his art. The two corresponded frequently. "You may come to get out of canvases what
I get out of sheets of paper," the father wrote in the spring of
1927. "I think the reason I want you to be an artist, have an
artist's point of view, is just because such times compensate for
so much else. . . . In art there is the possibility of impersonal
love. For modern men it is, I think, the only road to God. I presume that is why, loving you as my son, I want you to be an artist.
I don't really give a damn whether you succeed or not." John was
still in Paris, and Sherwood Anderson was back at his home in
Virginia, when the letter below was written:

[Troutdale, Virginia, ? April, 1927]

[No salutation]

Something I should have said in my letter yesterday.

In relation to painting.

Don't be carried off your feet by anything because it is
modern, the latest thing.

177

Go to the Louvre often and spend a good deal of time before the Rembrandts, the Delacroix's.

Learn to draw. Try to make your hand so unconsciously adept that it will put down what you feel without your having to think of your hands.

Then you can think of the thing before you.

Draw things that have some meaning to you. An apple, what does it mean?

The object drawn doesn't matter so much. It's what you feel about it, what it means to you.

A masterpiece could be made of a dish of turnips.

Draw, draw, hundreds of drawing[s].

Try to remain humble. Smartness kills everything.

The object of art is not to make salable pictures. It is to save yourself.

Any cleanness I have in my own life is due to my feeling for words.

The fools who write articles about me think that one morning I suddenly decided to write and began to produce masterpieces.

There is no special trick about writing or painting either. I wrote constantly for 15 years before I produced anything with any solidity to it.

For days, weeks, and months now I can't do it.

You saw me in Paris this winter. I was in a dead, blank time. You have to live through such times all your life.

The thing, of course, is to make yourself alive. Most people remain all of their lives in a stupor.

The point of being an artist is that you may live.

Such things as you suggested in your letter the other day. I said, "Don't do what you would be ashamed to tell me about."

I was wrong.

You can't depend on me. Don't do what you would be ashamed of before a sheet of white paper or a canvas.

The materials have to take the place of God.

About color. Be careful. Go to nature all you can. Instead of paintshops, other men's palettes, look at the sides of buildings in every light. Learn to observe little thing[s], a red apple lying on a grey cloth.

Trees, trees against [a] hill, everything. I know little enough. It seems to me that if I wanted to learn about color, I would try always to make a separation. There is a plowed field here before me, below it a meadow, half-decayed cornstalk[s] in the meadow making yellow lines, stumps, sometimes like looking into an ink bottle, sometimes almost blue.

The same in nature is a composition.

You look at it, thinking, "What made up that color?" I have walked over a piece of ground, after seeing it from a distance, trying to see what made the color I saw.

Light makes so much difference.

You won't arrive. It is an endless search.

I write as though you were a man. Well, you must know my heart is set on you.

It isn't your success I want. There is a possibility of your having a decent attitude toward people and work. That alone may make a man of you.

[P.S.] . . . tell the man at the shop where you go for the Picasso book [that the Cezanne prints arrived], or if you have been there, drop him a note—the shop, I mean.

A decade later Anderson wrote to Gertrude Stein that John "has got a little house in the country and is painting. God knows what will best bring out the poet in such a young painter." His son's career was on his mind a good deal. Once he sent one of John's canvases to his friend Alfred Stieglitz, the art critic and husband of Georgia O'Keeffe. "I wanted to get his feeling about John's work to check with my own. He says some pretty fine things, speaking of his fine color sense and most of all of a kind of boldness and directness . . . what is happening to John is O.K."

V

*   *   *

Occasions of Moment

*. . . the fruits of knowledge
and the events they incur
. . . sometimes unpredictably.*

". . . tomorrow long I to go to God . . ."

Thomas More Addresses His Last Letter
to His Daughter:

For four years during his youth, Thomas More fasted, wore a hair shirt and submitted to the discipline of Carthusian monks. In the end, however, he turned to the law, and his great intellect was diverted to the service of the government. Then Cardinal Wolsey was deposed and Henry VIII named More as High Chancellor, counting on his support in achieving a divorce from Catherine of Aragon. Henry had misgauged his man, and Thomas More's destiny was sealed. More refused to accept the oath of supremacy and, after every effort was made to shake his constancy, he was executed on July 6, 1535. Below, directed to his daughter Margaret, is the last letter he ever wrote, which breaks off abruptly as if interrupted by the executioner's summons:

[July 5, 1535]

Our Lord bless you, good daughter, and your good husband, and your little boy, and all yours, and all my children, and all my God-children, and all our friends. Recommend me when ye may, to my good daughter Cecily, whom I beseech our Lord to comfort. And I send her my blessing and to all her children, and pray her to pray for me. I send her an handkercher: and God comfort my good son her husband. My good daughter Daunce hath the picture in parchment, that you delivered me from my lady Coniers, her name is on the back-side. Show her that I heartily pray her that you may send it in my name to her again, for a token from me to pray for me. I like special well Dorothy Colley [his daughter's maid], I pray you to be good unto her. I would wit whether this be she that you wrote me of.

If not yet I pray you be good to the other as you may in her affliction, and to my good daughter Joan Aleyn too. Give her I pray some kind answer, for she sued hither to me this day to pray you be good to her. I cumber you good Margaret much, but I would be sorry, if it should be any longer than tomorrow. For it is Saint Thomas even, and the octave of Saint Peter: and therefore tomorrow long I to go to God: it were a day very meet and convenient for me. I never liked your manner toward me better, than when you kissed me last: for I love when daughterly love and dear charity hath no leisure to look to worldly courtesy. Farewell my dear child, and pray for me, and I shall for you and all your friends, that we may merrily meet in heaven. I thank you for your great cost. I send now my good daughter Clement her algorism stone [apparently a slate], and I send her my godson and all hers, God's blessing and mine. I pray you at time convenient recommend me to my good son John More. I liked well his natural fashion. Our Lord bless him and his good wife my loving daughter, to whom I pray him to be good as he hath great cause: and that if the land of mine come to his hand, he break not my will concerning his sister Daunce. And our Lord bless Thomas and Austin and all that they shall have. . . .

His letter unfinished, Sir Thomas went next day to the block. His head was fixed upon London Bridge, and tradition says it was rescued by the daughter to whom this letter was written, and that it was buried with her at St. Dunstan's, Canterbury. More was beatified in 1886, and canonized by Pope Pius XI.

* * *

Paul Revere, After His Midnight Ride, Tells His Son to Wait:

For ten days after he sounded the alarm that alerted the Minute
Men, Paul Revere was cut off from his family, virtually hiding
out in Cambridge during the day, and risking capture at night
as he rode through the dark, delivering urgent messages. When
he left Cambridge for Charlestown, he managed to get instructions
through to his wife, telling her how to join him. But his eldest
son was fifteen, and Revere expected the boy to stay behind and
look after the shop that had had to be abandoned just before
the Battle of Lexington. In his message to his wife, Revere said,
"Tell Paul I expect he'l behave himself well and attend to my
business, and not be out of the way." He wrote even more firmly
to the boy:

[Late in April, 1775]

My Son.

    It is now in your power to be serviceable to me, your Mother
and yourself. I beg you will keep yourself at home or where
your Mother sends you. Dont come away till I send you word.
When you bring anything to the ferry tell them its mine & mark
it with my name.

Your loving Father
P. R.

*   *   *

Horatio Nelson Receives His Father's Congratulations:

It was after the Battle of St. Vincent, on February 14, 1797, that Horatio Nelson skyrocketed into the public consciousness of England. He had led the assault that resulted in a sweeping victory over the Spanish fleet in the West Indies, and the courageous skill that was to become his trade-mark was hailed for the first time outside the Navy. Nelson's daring was such that all who knew him worried about his safety; indeed, it was five months after this letter from his father that he left his ship to direct the attack on Santa Cruz from a boat, and thereby lost his arm. Edmund Nelson, a parish vicar, describes below the feelings of a father whose son has become a hero.

[February 1797]

I thank God with all the power of a grateful soul, for the mercies he has most graciously bestowed on me, in preserving you amidst the imminent perils which so lately threatened your life at every moment; and amongst other innumerable blessings, I must not forget the bounty of Heaven in granting you a mind that rejoices in the practice of those eminent virtues which form great and good characters. Not only my few acquaintances here, but the people in general met me at every corner with such handsome words, that I was obliged to retire from the public eye. A wise Moralist has observed, that even bliss can rise to a certain pitch; and this has been verified in me. The height of glory to which your professional judgement, united with a proper degree of bravery, guarded by Providence, has raised you, few sons, my dear child, attain to, and few fathers live to see. Tears of joy

186

have involuntarily trickled down my furrowed cheek. Who could stand the force of such general congratulation? The name and service of Nelson have sounded throughout the City of Bath, from the common ballad-singer to the public theatre. Joy sparkles in every eye, and desponding Britain draws back her sable veil, and smiles. It gives me inward satisfaction to know, that the laurels you have wreathed sprang from those principles and religious truths which alone constitute the Hero; and though a Civic Crown is all you at present reap, it is to the mind of inestimable value, and I have no doubt will one day bear a golden apple: that field of glory, in which you have long been so conspicuous, is still open. May God continue to be your preserver from the arrow that flieth by day, and the pestilence that walketh by night.

*　　*　　*

*". . . as one might watch from a rock
the wreck of whole fleets."*

Goethe Writes to His Son on the Day After a Great Battle:

After Napoleon and Goethe met at Erfurt in the spring of 1813, the embattled emperor turned to a companion and said of Goethe, *"Voila un homme!"* The admiration was mutual. Goethe had little sympathy for the Prussian war for liberation, and he regarded Napoleon as the defender of civilization against the barbarism of the Slavs. He was visiting a Bohemian spa when Bonaparte scored his hollow triumph in the nearby battle of Bautzen, and this note, written to his son, August, on the following day, reflects his lack of concern for the success of his fellow Germans.

Teplitz
22nd May 1813

I had already sealed the enclosed when this ballad (to be called "The Walking Bell") came into being. So I am hurrying to send it too, for I hope you will like your invention in this guise. With it I am sending for Prince Bernhard that famous "Dance of Death" as a ballad. You can always exchange it for the "Walking Bell." And here's also a little blue landscape that some good friend can smooth out and mount for you on paper. These bits of fun will serve the important purpose, too, of telling you to be happy and cheerful in whatever your present day-to-day circumstances are. For the disaster that is happening near us is measureless, and we watch it in safety but with trepidation, as one might watch from a rock the wreck of whole fleets. Farewell . . . My love to you, and enjoy every reasonably good hour . . . life would be unbearable here in Teplitz if the sun didn't shine longer than usual; yet one is bored enough.

August von Goethe, at the age of sixteen, served as a witness when his father finally married his mother in 1806, and the two were very close throughout the son's life. When August died suddenly in 1830, the poet said through his tears, *"Non ignoravi, me mortalem genuisse!"* [I knew that I had begotten a mortal.] On the monument for the young man's grave, Goethe caused these words to be carved: Goethe, Fil. Patri. Antevertens. Obit.

188

Annorium. XL. MDCCCXXX. [Goethe, the son, preceding his
father, died at the age of forty in 1830.]

*   *   *

". . . fetch me away from this Bastile . . ."

John Clare Asks His Sixteen-Year-Old Son
for Freedom:

Though he began to show signs of insanity while still a young
man, John Clare was forever struggling to live normally with his
family. Once he set out to walk all the way home from a private
sanitarium. After that he was committed to the Northampton
general lunatic asylum northwest of London. Through it all he
continued to write poetry and to concern himself with his
children. He had always been ambitious for their minds, for he
wished to free them from the ignorance of the class from which,
as he once said, he himself had "struggled upward as one struggling
from the nightmare in his sleep." His letters are studded with
the urgency he felt. "I tell you all Brothers & Sisters to love
truth be Honest & fear Nobody—Amuse yourselves in reading
& writing—you all have the Bible and other suitable books—I
would advise you to study Mathematics Astronomy Languages &
Botony as the best amusements for instruction—Angling is a
Recreation I was fond of myself & there is no harm in it if
your taste is the same." The letter below was written fifteen
years before he was released from the asylum by death.

Nov 7th [1849]
Asylum
Northampton

My dear Charles

I ought to have answered your Letter before now but I have to go down below for Ink & Paper & forgot all about it till this Morning—You never tell me my dear Boy when I am to come Home I have been here Nine years or Nearly & want to come Home very much—You need not mind about writing often only in your next say when Johnny is coming to fetch me away from this Bastile—Have you four Boys got each an Hebrew Bible & a Harry Phillips on Angling—How do you get on with the Flowers—how are your Sisters & your Mother & Grandfather your Three Brothers & your Neighbours Give my Love to them all & Helpston People likewise—Take care of my Books & M.S.S. till I come—to your Neighbours on each side of you give my best respects—& to Mary Buzley & old Mr Buzley if alive —& believe me my dear Son

Your affectionate Father
John Clare

*   *   *

James Fenimore Cooper Encourages a Daughter's Literary Debut:

The man who wrote the *Leatherstocking Tales* was above all a father. He was no more able to view his offspring's ability objectively than most parents. When his daughter Susan produced a book-length manuscript, he looked for the best in it, and did everything possible to use his business talent to her advantage. True, it took him seven years to bring about publication, but his delight in the outcome is so genuine as to make his lack of critical ability the more lovely.

Globe, Feb. 28th, 1850

My dear Sue,

I cannot let the occasion pass without expressing to you the great satisfaction I have had in reading the sheets [of *Rural Hours*]. So far from finding them disjointed and tame, they carried me along with the interest of a tale. The purity of mind, the simplicity, elegance, and knowledge they manifest, must, I think, produce a strong feeling in your favor with all the pure and good. I have now very little doubt of its ultimate success, though at first the American world will hesitate to decide.

I shall see that the sheets are sent to England, where I should think its success would be marked. The unfortunate state of the copyright law may prevent your receiving much remuneration, though it must produce something. . . .

I have read the sheets twice, and with real pleasure. You have picked up a great deal of information, and imparted it in a very polished way.

Adieu, my beloved child—the success of your book is much

191

nearer my heart than that of my own, and I own I am not without hopes for you, while I have little or none for myself.

Give my tenderest regards to your sisters—as for Ma-tie [Mrs. Cooper], I shall tell her my own story.

Yours very affectionately,

J. Fenimore Cooper.

What Cooper told Ma-tie was that their daughter's book was "not strong perhaps, but is so pure, and so elegant, so very feminine and charming, that I do not doubt now, of its eventual success—I say *eventual*, for, at first the world will not know what to make of it. . . . She has struggled nobly, and deserves success. At any rate, she has pleased us, and that is a great deal for so dear a child." Cooper was more than pleased when Washington Irving made haste to congratulate him on his daughter's publication; William Cullen Bryant insisted that *Rural Hours* was "a great book—the greatest of the season, and a credit to the country," and a magazine reviewer compared it to the work of the Brontë sisters. "Right and left," Cooper reported to his wife, "I hear of *Rural Hours*. I am stopped in the street a dozen times a day to congratulate me."

✻ ✻ ✻

John Brown Urges His Family to Abhor Slavery with Undying Hatred:

John Brown, said Wendell Phillips, had "Letters of marque from God." After his conviction of "treason, and conspiring and advising with slaves and other rebels, and murder in the first degree," he was imprisoned and sentenced to be hanged. The day before the execution was scheduled, he asked permission to spend his last night on earth with his wife, and was refused by the commanding general. Quelling his passionate anger, Brown sat down and wrote his farewell to all his family, calling on his children to teach his precepts to their children and their children's children.

Charlestown, Prison, Jefferson Co., Va.
30th Nov 1859
My dearly beloved wife, Sons: & Daughters, Everyone

As I now begin what is probably the last letter I shall ever write to any of you; I conclude to write you all at the same time. . . . I am waiting the hour of my public *murder* with great composure of mind, & cheerfulness: feeling the strongest assurance that in no other possible way could I be used to so much advance the cause of God; & of humanity: & that nothing that either I or all my family have sacrificed or suffered: *will be lost.*

The reflection that a wise & merciful, *as well as just* & *holy God:* rules not only the affairs of *this world;* but of all worlds; is a rock to set our feet upon; under all circumstances: *even* those more severely *trying ones:* into which our own follies; & rongs have placed us. I have no doubt that our seeming *disaster:*

will ultimately result in the most *glorious success*. So my dear *shattered* & *broken* family be of good cheer; & believe & trust in God; *"With all your heart & with all your soul"*; for *"he* doeth *All things well."* Do not feel ashamed on my account; nor *for one moment* despair of the cause; or grow *weary of well doing*. I bless God; I never felt stronger confidence in the certain and near approach of a *bright Morning*; & a *glorious day*; than I have felt; & do now feel; since my confinement here.

I am endeavouring to "return" like a "poor Prodgal" *as I am*, to my Father: against whom I have *always* sined: *in the hope;* that he may kindly, & forgivingly "meet me: though *a verry great way off."* Oh my dear Wife & Children would "to God" you could know how I have been "travelling in birth for you" *all:* that no one of you "may fail of the grace of God, through Jesus Christ:" that no one of you may be blind to the truth: & glorious "light of *his* word," in which Life; & Immortality; are brought to light.

I beseech you *every one* to make the bible your *dayly & Nightly study;* with a *childlike honest, candid, teachable spirit:* out of love and respect for your husband; & Father: & I beseech *the God of my Fathers;* to open all your eyes to a discovery of *the truth.* You *cannot imagine* how much *you* may *soon need* the consolations of the Christian religion.

Circumstances like my own; for more than a month past; convince me beyond *all doubt:* of our great *need:* of something more to rest our hopes on; than merely our own vague theories framed up, while our *prejudices* are excited; *or* our *vanity* worked up to its highest pitch.

Oh do not trust your eternal all upon the boisterous Ocean, without *even* a *Helm;* or *Compass* to *aid* you in steering. I do *not* ask *any* of you; to throw *away your reason:* I only *ask* you, to make a candid & sober *use of your reason:* My dear younger children will you listen to the last poor admonition of one who can only love you? Oh be determined at once to give your whole hearts to God; & let *nothing* shake; or alter; that resolution. You need have no fear *of regreting it.*

Do not be vain; and thoughtless: but *sober minded.* And let me entreat you all to love *the whole remnant* of our once great family: "with a pure *heart fervently."* Try to *build again:* your broken walls: & to make *the utmost* of every *stone* that is left. Nothing can so tend to make life a blessing as the consciousness that you *love: & are beloved:* & "love ye the stranger" *still.* It is ground of the utmost comfort to *my* mind: to know that so many of you as have had *the opportunity;* have given full proof of your fidelity to the great family of man.

Be faithful until death. From the exercise of habitual love to man: *it cannot* be very *hard:* to *learn to love* his *maker. I* must yet insert a reason for my firm belief in the Divine inspiration of the Bible: notwithstanding I am (perhaps naturally) skeptical: (certainly not, credulous.) I wish you all to consider *it most thoroughly;* when you read the blessed book; & see whether you *can not* discover such evidence yourselves. It is the purity of *heart, feeling, or motive:* as well as *word, & action* which is everywhere insisted on; that distinguish it from *all other teachings;* that *commends* it to *my conscience;* whether *my heart* be "willing, & obedient" *or not.* The inducements that it holds out; are another reason *of my conviction* of its *truth;* & *genuineness:* that I cannot here *omit;* in this my *last argument* for the Bible.

Eternal life; is that my soul *is "panting after" this moment.* I mention this; as reason for endeavouring to leave a valuable copy of the Bible to be carefully *preserved* in remembrance of *me:* to so many of my posterity; *instead* of some other things of equal cost.

I beseech you all to live in habitual contentment with verry *moderate* circumstances: & gains, of worldly store: & most earnestly to teach this: to your *children; & Childrens Children;* after you: by *example:* as well; as precept. Be determined to know by experience as *soon as may be:* whether bible instruction is of *Divine origin* or not; *which says; "Owe no man anything but* to love one another." John Rogers wrote to his children, "Abhor the arrant whore of Rome." John Brown writes to his children to Abhor with *undiing hatred,* also: that "sum of vilainies;" Slavery.

Remember that "he that is *slow* to *anger* is *better* than the mighty: and he that ruleth his spirit; than he that taketh a city." Remember also: *that* "they that be *wise* shall *shine;* and they that *turn* many to *righteousness:* as the stars forever; & ever." And now dearly beloved Farewell, To God & the word of his grace I comme[n]d you all.

Your Affectionate Husband & Father
John Brown

* * *

Lee's Return to a Scene of Battle Is Reported to His Son:

Of William H. Fitzhugh Lee, the recipient of this letter, it was said that "he was too big to be a man but not big enough to be a horse." He served in his father's army as a cavalry commander under Jeb Stuart and was wounded before Gettysburg, then captured. As a result, he did not take part in the campaign Robert E. Lee alludes to below.

Lexington, Virginia, December 21, 1867

My dear Fitzhugh: . . . My visit to Petersburg was extremely pleasant. Besides the pleasure of seeing my daughter and being with you, which was very great, I was gratified in seeing many friends. In addition, when our armies were in front of Petersburg I suffered so much in body and mind on account of the good townspeople, especially on that gloomy night when I was forced to abandon them, that I have always reverted to them in sadness and sorrow. My old feelings returned to me, as I passed well-remembered spots and recalled the ravages of the hostile shells. But when I saw the cheerfulness with which the people were working to restore their condition, and witnessed the comforts with which they were surrounded, a load of sorrow which had been pressing upon me for years was lifted from my heart. This is bad weather for completing your house, but it will soon pass away, and your sweet helpmate will make everything go smoothly. When the spring opens and the mocking-birds resume their song you will have much to do. So you must prepare in time. . . . God bless you all is the prayer of

Your devoted father,
R. E. Lee

It was at Petersburg that Lee made his last stand. His men took a four-day battering from Grant in the summer of 1864, and the following spring Lee tried to break through the besieging army by an unsuccessful attack on nearby Fort Stedman. On April second, Lee evacuated Petersburg and Richmond, and a week later he had no choice but to meet Grant at Appomattox Court House. In the peace that followed, both father and son helped to persuade their fellow Virginians to be loyal Americans—the general as president of what is now Washington and Lee University, and Fitzhugh Lee as a member of the United States House of Representatives.

*　　*　　*

"Rejoice, my children!"

Louis Pasteur Announces a Great Discovery:

Millions of sheep and cattle throughout the world were dying of anthrax when Pasteur started his experiments on the disease's cause and cure. Though he was already highly respected by the medical profession, his very success caused bitter jealousy among some of his contemporaries who cast aspersions on his anthrax work. To quiet the taunts, Pasteur arranged to have a public test of his immunization method. After fifty sheep had been inoculated, however, he became uneasy—observers had noted

198

that some of the vaccinated animals had temperatures. Doubt suddenly overwhelmed Pasteur, and he told his wife that he wished he could crawl into a dark corner. "This will be the ruin of all my work and all my hopes!" he cried. Then, after a night of anxiety, the message he here describes to his children came from the farm where the test had been staged.

June 2, 1881

It is only Thursday, and I am already writing to you; it is because a great result is now acquired. A wire from Melun has just announced it. On Tuesday last, May 31, we inoculated all the sheep, vaccinated and nonvaccinated, with a very virulent splenic fever. It is not forty-eight hours ago. Well, the telegram tells me that, when we arrive at two o'clock this afternoon, all the nonvaccinated subjects will be dead; eighteen were already dead this morning, the others dying. As to the vaccinated ones, they are all well; the telegram ends by the words, "stunning success"; it is from the veterinary surgeon, M. Rossignol.

It is too early yet for a final judgment; the vaccinated sheep might yet fall ill. But when I write to you on Sunday, if all goes well, it may be taken for granted that they will henceforth preserve their good health, and that the success will indeed have been startling. On Tuesday, we had a foretaste of the final results. On Saturday and Sunday, two sheep had been abstracted from the lot of twenty-five vaccinated sheep, and two from the lot of twenty-five nonvaccinated ones, and inoculated with a very virulent virus. Now, when on Tuesday all the visitors arrived, amongst whom were M. Tisserand, M. Patinot, the Prefect of Seine-et-Marne, M. Foucher de Careil, Senator, etc., we found the two unvaccinated sheep dead, and the two others in good health.

I then said to one of the veterinary surgeons who were present, "Did I not read in a newspaper, signed by you, apropos of the virulent organism of saliva, " 'There! one more microbe; when there are 100 we shall make a cross'?" "It is true," he immediately answered, honestly. "But I am a converted and repentant sinner." "Well," I answered, "allow me to remind you of the words of the Gospel: joy shall be in heaven over one sinner that repenteth, more than over ninety and nine just persons which need no repentance." Another veterinary surgeon who was present said, "I will bring you another, M. Colin." "You are mistaken," I replied. "M. Colin contradicts for the sake of contradicting, and does not believe because he will not believe. You would have to cure a case of nuerosis, and you cannot do that!" Joy reigns in the laboratory and in the house. Rejoice, my children!

Pasteur's children were very close to their father, and were often assistants in his experiments. Once he summed up his feeling about his family in a letter to his wife: "I wish that after my return there should be between us and with us nothing but our love, our children, their education and their future, together with my dreams as a scientist."

*　　　*　　　*

". . . up to the end I was in a funk."

Anthony Trollope Cheers His Son's Election to an Exclusive Club:

Henry Merivale Trollope was surrounded by a family of writers. He grew up to receive the fond coaching of his father, Anthony, and the example of an uncle, an aunt and a grandmother. But for all the printer's ink that ran in his blood, Henry failed to achieve the success of his elders. His father's letters to him are laced with advice on style and the repeated admonition not to submit slovenly work. Throughout the correspondence between father and son there is the strong current of Anthony Trollope's affection for his offspring and his half-hidden worry about the young man's success. The urgency with which he wanted his son's acceptance in the London literary world was never clearer than when he sought membership for him in The Athenaeum Club, founded by Sir Walter Scott—election to which was one of Britain's most coveted distinctions.

Athenaeum Club
13 February 1882

Dear Harry

You have been elected by 204 votes to 4—I have not heard of so overpowering a majority. They tell me here that they do not know of anything like it. However you are now a member of the Athenaeum.

God bless you
Your own father
A. T.

Three days later the father was still full of the victory.

[Harting, Petersfield.]

16—Feb—1882
Dear Harry,

It was a jolly triumph. I was awfully nervous. But when the balloting began the Secretary came to me and told me that you would certainly get in. Knowing the club so well I suppose he understands all the whisperings. I remained there—as did Millais. And we did the best we could. Nevertheless up to the end I was in a funk. When the bulletins came over at six o'clock

I retired into the card room as it was necessary I should remain somewhere to hear the news. At a quarter to 7 a dozen men backed by the Secretary came to me and told me the result. Somebody said that they had never remembered so large a majority. One blackball in 10 excludes,—but one in 50 would not have kept you out. I congratulate you with all my heart. I wrote immediately after the ballot, but it was too late for the post.

I dont expect you will ever condescend to look into the Garrick [club] again. Palgrave Simpson assured me, three times over, that he knew you very intimately at the Garrick. It's a great comfort to think that when it has been done once it has been done for ever.

There is a bundle of papers here which the Secretary has sent down for you, which can be kept for your arrival. The only one that means anything is a demand
for £31 = 10 = Entrance
and £ 8 = 8 = Subscription
$$\overline{£39 = 18}$$
which is £10 = 10 more than I had thought. But it shall be paid at once.

Yours most affectionately
A. T.

* * *

Robert Browning Applauds His Son's
Good Fortune:

On March 9, 1849, Robert Browning wrote to a friend: "Ba desires me to tell you that she gave birth, at 2¼ this morning, to a fine, strong boy, like Harry Gil with the voice of three— a fact we learned when he was about half born——" The boy, nicknamed "Penini," or "Pen," was twelve when his mother died, and always thereafter Robert Browning was concerned about his son's welfare. Pen failed to be accepted at Baliol, and gave up before he had finished at Christ Church. He was a very real problem to his father, who said that the boy might "want no end of money." He told another friend that "Pen won't work." To be better able to support his son, Browning went so far as to propose marriage to Louisa Lady Ashburton, a very rich widow, making it clear that "the attractiveness of a marriage with her lay in its advantages to Pen." His heart, Browning said, "was buried in Florence" with Elizabeth Barrett. Such candor brought rejection from Lady Ashburton, and the poet struggled to help his son's attempt to be a painter and sculptor until the fortunate event he discusses here:

Villa Berry, St. Moritz, Aug. 19, '87

Dearest Pen,—I waited for the letter in reply to my last,— which I knew would be on the way,—before answering the more important one—which took me by surprise indeed,—but a very joyful surprise. I think you could not do a wiser, better thing than marry the in every way suitable lady whom you have been fortunate enough to induce to take such a step, and who, you are bound to feel, behaves with the utmost generosity. You know very well I have never had any other aim than your happiness in all I have done: the kind of life you have been forced to lead

203

these last years always seemed comfortless and even dangerous to me,—whatever might be said for it as helpful to your art (and *that* it no doubt was)—you must know it had lasted long enough for the purpose, and could not, in the nature of things, continue as you advance in years: "no home"—is sad work,—and with a home, and *such* a home as [with] *such* a wife as yours will be, your further progress will be infinitely more easy and rapid. I do approve of your choice will all my heart: there is no young person I know at all comparable to Miss C. She has every requisite to make you happy and successful, if you deserve it—as I believe you will endeavour to do. If the lady had been unknown to me,—or one of the innumerable pleasant parties to a flirtation and utterly useless for anything else, I should have given you up for lost. As it is, you are at just the time of life when you may 'take a fresh departure' with the greatest advantage. You can bring all your acquired Continental knowledge to bear on an English enterprise: take a house and studio here, and try what may be done when your work may have the chance which you never yet enjoyed—of being seen, as you produce them, in your own Studio, with the advantage of acquaintance with all the artists you care to know. Miss C. has spoken to me with the greatest frankness and generosity of the means she will have of contributing to your support—for my part, I can engage to give you £300 a year: this, with the results of your work—if you manage to sell but a single picture in the year—will amply suffice. Of course, at my death you will have whatever I possess: and meantime if any good fortune comes to me—well, it will be, as it ever has been, your good fortune also.

I write very temperately about all this—but it makes me really happy—as I should not be, if I doubted you would not

do your utmost to deserve such a blessing as God seems disposed
to give you: may He bless you, I pray from my heart.

Ever affectionately yours
Robert Browning

✳   ✳   ✳

"I sealed the . . . treaty
with Lord Byron's ring . . ."

John Hay Describes a Moment
of American History:

Once secretary to Abraham Lincoln, John Hay was Theodore
Roosevelt's Secretary of State during the negotiations that resulted in the acquisition of the Panama Canal Zone. He had
spent the summer of 1903 trying to bring the long-debated canal
project into focus, and finally, after a revolution resulting in the
establishment of the Republic of Panama, had signed the Hay-
Bunau-Varilla Treaty, authorizing the United States to link the
Atlantic Ocean with the Pacific. His ability to share—in swift,
intimate sentences—a climactic moment is shown in a letter to
Mrs. Payne Whitney, his daughter.

Washington, November 19, 1903

As for your poor old dad, they are working him nights and
Sundays. I have never, I think, been so constantly and actively
employed as during the last fortnight. Yesterday morning the

negotiations with Panama were far from complete. But by putting on all steam, getting Root and Knox and Shaw together at lunch, I went over my project line by line, and fought out every section of it; adopted a few good suggestions; hurried back to the Department, set everybody at work drawing up final drafts —sent for Varilla, went over the whole treaty with him, explained all the changes, got his consent, and at seven o'clock signed the momentous document in the little blue drawing-room, out of Abraham Lincoln's inkstand, and with C—'s pen. Varilla had no seal, so he used mine. (Did I ever tell you I sealed the Hay-Herbert Treaty with Lord Byron's ring, having nothing else in the house?)

So that great job is ended—at least this stage of it. I have nothing else; will come up before Thanksgiving.

✳   ✳   ✳

". . . you write them with your heart."

General William Booth Gives Thanks for Letters on His Blindness:

In his eighty-third year, life ended for William Booth, founder of the Salvation Army and one of the great revivalists of modern times. Not long before his death, he lost his sight, but even this fact did not diminish his zeal. As Vachel Lindsay put it in "General William Booth Enters into Heaven":

Booth died blind and still by faith he trod,
Eyes still dazzled by the ways of God.
Booth led boldly, and he looked the chief,
Eagle countenance in sharp relief,
Beard a-flying, air of high command
Unabated in that holy land.

The General's blindness seemed a great blow to all those close to him—perhaps more to his daughter Evangeline than to anyone else. She was in command of the Salvation Army in America, and her father was at his home in London when he wrote:

July 20, 1912

I had your letter. Bless you a thousand times! You are a lovely correspondent. You don't write your letters with your pen, or with your tongue, you write them with your heart. Hearts are different; some, I suppose, are born sound and musical, others are born uncertain and unmusical, and are at best a mere tinkling cymbal. Yours, I have no doubt, has blessed and cheered and delighted the soul of the mother who bore you from the very first opening of your eyes upon the world, and that dear heart has gone on with that cheering influence from that time to the present, and it will go on cheering everybody around you who has loved you, and it will go on cheering among the rest of your loving brother Branwell and your devoted General right away to the end; nay will go on endlessly, for there is to be no conclusion to our affection.

I want it to be so. I want it to be my own experience. Love, to be a blessing, must be ambitious, boundless, and eternal. O Lord, help me! and O Lord, destroy everything in me that interferes with the prosperity, growth, and fruitfulness of this precious, divine, and everlasting fruit!

I have been ill—I have been very ill indeed. I have had a return of my indigestion in its most terrible form. This spasmodic feeling of suffocation has so distressed me that at times it has seemed almost impossible for me to exist. Still, I have fought my way through, and the doctors this afternoon have told me as bluntly and plainly as an opinion could be given to a man, that I must struggle on and not give way, or the consequence will be very serious.

Then, too, the eye has caused me much pain, but that has very much, if not entirely, passed off, and the occulist tells me that the eye will heal up. But alas! alas! I am absolutely blind. It is very painful, but I am not the only blind man in the world, and I can easily see how, if I am spared, I shall be able to do a good deal of valuable work.

So I am going to make another attempt at work. What do you think of that? I have sat down this afternoon, not exactly to the desk, but anyway to the duties of the desk, and I am going to strive to stick to them if I possibly can. I have been down to some of my meals; I have had a walk in the garden, and now it is proposed for me to take a drive in a motor, I believe some kind soul is loaning me. Anyhow, I am going to have some machine that will shuffle me along the street, road, and square, and I will see how that acts on my nerves, and then perhaps try something more.

However, I am going into action once more in the Salvation War, and I believe, feeble as I am, God is going to give me another good turn, and another blessed wave of success.

You will pray for me. I would like before I die—it has been one of the choicest wishes of my soul—to be able to make the Salvation Army such a power for God and of such benefit to mankind that no wicked people can spoil it. . . .

Each of General Booth's children had become an officer in the Salvation Army, and their father made them understand (as he wrote in his journal in 1893) "that they must conform to Orders and Regulations as other Officers, that I am *General* first and Father afterwards." Such military discipline served only to increase the devotion of his daughter Eva. She wrote to him, "You know my love for you, my ever-burning, all-absorbing desire to please you in every particular, to comfort you, to help you, and in some small measure to brighten the other end of life's journey for you, to live in your heart, and to spend every energy in the front ranks of the battle that you are waging." She signed herself, "Ever in fondest and unchanging love, Your own little soldier child."

*   *   *

". . . right with you with love
and with open heart . . ."

Nicola Sacco Speaks to His Children
as He Faces Execution:

Two Italian immigrants, a shoemaker and a fish-pedler, were found guilty in 1921 of the murder of two men who were carrying a payroll. In 1959, their conviction was still so much in doubt that a Massachusetts legislator made an effort to bring about a posthumous acquittal. In the intervening decades there were many who believed that Sacco and Vanzetti had been made scapegoats for an unsolved murder because they voiced political ideas unpopular in the community in which they lived. Bartolomeo Vanzetti tried to sum up the case in a letter to Nicola Sacco's thirteen-year-old son Dante: "I tell you now that I know your father, he is not a criminal, but one of the bravest men I ever knew. . . ." Appeals had failed for both men when Dante's father wrote less than a week before the end:

August 18, 1927. Charlestown State Prison
My dear Son and Companion:

Since the day I saw you last I had always the idea to write you this letter, but the length of my hunger strike and the thought I might not be able to explain myself, made me put it off all this time.

The other day, I ended my hunger strike and just as soon as I did that I thought of you to write to you, but I find that I did not have enough strength and I cannot finish it at one time. However, I want to get it down in any way before they take us again to the death house, because it is my conviction that just as soon as the court refuses a new trial to us they will take us there. And between Friday and Monday, if nothing happens, they will electrocute us right after midnight, on August 22nd. Therefore, here I am, right with you with love and with open heart as ever I was yesterday.

I never thought that our inseparable life could be separated, but the thought of seven dolorous years makes it seem it did come, but then it has not changed really the unrest and the heart-beat of affection. That has remained as it was. More. I say that our ineffable affection reciprocal, is today more than any other time, of course. That is not only a great deal but it is grand because you can see the real brotherly love, not only in joy but also and more in the struggle of suffering. Remember this, Dante. We have demonstrated this, and modesty apart we are proud of it.

Much we have suffered during this long Calvary. We protest today as we protested yesterday. We protest always for our freedom.

If I stopped hunger strike the other day, it was because there was no more sign of life in me. Because I protested with my hunger strike yesterday as today I protest for life and not for death.

I sacrificed because I wanted to come back to the embrace of your dear little sister Ines and your mother and all the beloved friends and comrades of life and not death. So Son, today life begins to revive slow and calm, but yet without horizon and always with sadness and visions of death.

Well, my dear boy, after your mother had talked to me so much and I had dreamed of you day and night, how joyful it was to see you at last. To have talked with you like we used to in the days—in those days. Much I told you on that visit and more I wanted to say, but I saw that you will remain the same affectionate boy, faithful to your mother who loves you so much, and I did not want to hurt your sensibilities any longer, because I am sure that you will continue to be the same boy and remember what I have told you. I know that and what here I am going to tell you will touch your sensibilities, but don't cry Dante, because many tears have been wasted, as your mother's have been wasted for seven years, and never did any good. So, Son, instead of crying, be strong, so as to be able to comfort your mother, and when you want to distract your mother from the discouraging soulness, I will tell you what I used to do. To take her for a long walk in the quiet country, gathering wild flowers here and there, resting under the shade of trees, between the harmony of the vivid stream and the gentle tranquility of the mother-nature [sic], and I am sure that she will enjoy this very much,

211

as you surely would be happy for it. But remember always, Dante, in the play of happiness, don't use all for yourself only, but down yourself just one step, at your side and help the weak ones that cry for help, help the prosecuted and the victim, because that are your better friends; they are the comrades that fight and fall as your father and Bartolo fought and fell yesterday for the conquest of the joy of freedom for all and the poor workers. In this struggle of life you will find more love and you will be loved.

I am sure that from what your mother told me about what you said during these last terrible days when I was lying in the iniquitous death-house—that description gave me happiness because it showed you will be the beloved boy I had always dreamed.

Therefore whatever should happen tomorrow, nobody knows, but if they should kill us, you must not forget to look at your friends and comrades with the smiling gaze of gratitude as you look at your beloved ones, because they love you as they love every one of the fallen persecuted comrades. I tell you, your father that is all the life to you, your father that loved you and saw them, and knows their noble faith (that is mine) their supreme sacrifice that they are still doing for our freedom, for I have fought with them, and they are the ones that still hold the last of our hope that today they can still save us from electrocution, it is the struggle and fight between the rich and the poor for safety and freedom, Son, which you will understand in the future of your years to come, of this unrest and struggle of life's death.

Much I thought of you when I was lying in the death-house —the singing, the kind tender voices of the children from the playground, where there was all the life and the joy of liberty

—just one step from the wall which contains the buried agony of three buried souls. It would remind me so often of you and your sister Ines, and I wish I could see you every moment. But I feel better that you did not come to the death-house so that you could not see the horrible picture of three lying in agony to be electrocuted, because I do not know what effect it would have on your young age. But then, in another way if you were not so sensitive it would be very useful to you tomorrow when you could use this horrible memory to hold up to the world the shame of the country in this cruel persecution and unjust death. Yes, Dante, they can crucify our bodies today as they are doing, but they cannot destroy our ideas, that will remain for the youth of the future to come.

Dante, when I said three human lives buried, I meant to say that with us there is another a young man by the name of Celestino Maderios that is to be electrocuted at the same time with us. He has been twice before in that horrible death-house, that should be destroyed with the hammers of real progress— that horrible house that will shame forever the future of the citizens of Massachusetts. They should destroy that house and put up a factory or school, to teach many of the hundreds of the poor orphan boys of the world.

Dante, I say once more to love and be nearest your mother and the beloved ones in these sad days, and I am sure that with your brave heart and kind goodness they will feel less discomfort. And you will also not forget to love me a little for I do— O, Sonny! thinking so much and so often of you.

Best fraternal greetings to the beloved ones, love and kisses to your little Ines and mother. Most hearty affectionate embrace.

Your Father and Companion

2 1 3

P. S.   Bartolo sends you the most affectionate greetings. I hope
that your mother will help you to understand this letter because
I could have written much better and more simple, if I was feeling good. But I am so weak.

*   *   *

*". . . I could no longer live
in music during the disasters . . ."*

Ernest Bloch to Suzanne Bloch at the Beginning of World War II:

The Swiss composer, Ernest Bloch, brought his family to America
in 1916 and stayed for the rest of his life. Here he wrote his
opera *Jézabel,* the *Second Quartette,* the *Rhapsodie hebraique*
and the symphony *America.* When the Second World War came,
he was in the American West that he loved, but his lifelong friends
were caught in the debacle of Europe. His letter to his daughter,
herself a distinguished musician, is eloquent in revealing an
artist's sensitivity to the events of his time.

Oswego, Oregon, July 24, 1940

My dear Suzanne:

I arrived here five days ago, after a fine and leisurely trip
as you will have learned from my cards. After Crater Lake,
which is *superb,* I spent two or three days at Diamond Lake, also
magnificent, and Mother and I may perhaps go there for several
weeks—then to another enchanting spot, Suttle Lake, and via

214

McKenzie Pass to the incredible Lava Beds—Eugene and Oregon.

This trip has done me more good than anything else. I made a complete recovery en route, regaining my energies and some weight (I had lost 10 pounds in 15 days). And most important —I managed to forget a little the nightmare of the recent news and developments, which had completely crushed and overwhelmed me. . . . A more general view of things, more cosmic and historical—frightful as things are—has gradually taken the place of the atrocious vision of the present. . . . The spiritual values and the progressive but slow advance of humanity cannot be destroyed even if current developments were to obliterate them. . . . Alas for those who live in these times, especially the victims! I am thinking of them all, my family in Geneva, my friends everywhere. You have to read their letters between the lines; the major part is censored. One understands that it is horrible and that the papers here don't give us even a hundredth of it.

On arrival I found your good letter of the 8th, and shortly after, your letter of the 19th arrived. Both of them are so consoling, so full of health and harmony, with the comforting view of your life, of this beautiful country, of Paul's work and yours, of Matthew, who seems to have such a delicate, dreamy nature and is certainly very gifted in music. I, too, suffer from being so far from you and from not being able to follow the developments of my little friend, but the main thing is that he is coming along so well.

While I am writing to you, Jodi woke up and he is making up a long conversation out of his head—it's priceless! Marianne has gone to lunch with some unexpected visitors at Oswego. Ivan was supposed to have left for Washington yesterday, by plane.

(I live across from them with some neighbors who put a room at my disposal.) I have developed my films and am gradually getting round to a large correspondence which has been waiting for me. I also read your letters to the family, and really, all of them breathe forth such a healthy, normal atmosphere, it rejoices me. Thank you also for your good wishes. Yes, sixty years old! That's the way the wheel turns, for all of us, and for the world.

In this quiet spot I hope to take up my work again, which was interrupted at the "Eroica" and the comparative studies. That in itself helps maintain one's equilibrium. The first part had been finished—40 pages! I had started the second, an enormous task, but passionately interesting . . . one redoes, backwards, all the work of Beethoven and one follows his mind and his heart—one goes into ecstasies over his superb *technique* (despite Nadia Boulanger), and the infallible logic that guides him. I have discovered (after 45 years of study) a thousand details that had escaped me up to now . . . it is a whole world—and the *step* between the Second Symphony and this one is the greatest a composer has ever taken! The orchestration, too, is a miracle of sobriety, invention, imagination, and *mastery*. From the standpoint of *rhythm* it is *incomparable!* Frequently there are seven or eight sketches for a passage or even more (Nottebohm does not give them all). I have copied all of them in different colors of ink above the *final version;* beneath is the final version on two, three, or four lines, depending on the case, and below that the tonal and rhythmic analysis—the punctuation. This comparative study is extraordinary, a lesson every hour, in each measure! You can sometimes see in it, after the most unbelievable groping, the development of all of Beethoven's thinking.

I had also begun, I believe I told you, a new quartet. I had to interrupt it when I could no longer live in music during the disasters in Europe—the collapse of all those values which constituted my life, our lives. But the first part (*lente*) is finished, and I believe it is something completely "new." There is no thematic development, no tonal restrictions, no *repetition* of motifs—and still the "story" unfolds with absolute logic and *organic continuity*. Why? I don't know. I do not know any literary work that even comes close to it. If I can succeed in writing the whole quartet this way, it will be extraordinary, a complete regeneration of my style—(though it's pure Bloch). With this I stop.

Today I developed five films; moments like these are "holiday feasts" greeted with a hearty appetite.

Have a nice vacation, don't work too hard, take care of yourself, and store up some air and sunshine and energy for the winter. You are right. One must ignore the musical world so far as possible. It is only, alas, that one knows what *real* music is, detached from all the vanity and irrelevancy that have nothing to do with the ART itself. It's probably the same way in everything. On the trip I ran into several people here and there who were very intelligent and cordial and they bore witness of the finest side of America, far from these radios and newspapers.

Regards to Paul, I kiss you and the baby, with all my heart,
Ernest

*   *   *

General Eisenhower Takes Time for a Letter in a Sicilian Tunnel:

The invasion of Sicily during World War II was only a few days old when Dwight D. Eisenhower paused to write a birthday letter to his son. Eisenhower at this time, according to John Gunther, "was working in a damp cubicle not bigger than ten feet by fourteen; there was a single table covered by a gray blanket and a white blotter; an oil heater was burning, but the clay floor was wet and cold. The General tossed away one of his cigarettes and asked, 'You fellows got a dry cigarette?' None of us had." In this setting, Ike wrote as follows, dated July 12, 1943:

Dear Johnnie: This is written from my advanced C. P. during the early days of the Sicilian attack. The papers keep you fairly well informed of our operations, so you know that this whole force is hard at it again.

Strangely enough, for me personally, the beginning of one of these major pushes is a period of comparative inactivity, because there is so much waiting for reports, while I'm removed from my main headquarters where there is always something to keep one hustling.

The main purpose of this note is to wish you well on your birthday. You will be twenty-one—a voter if you were a civilian! I wish I could be there to shake you by the hand and say "Good luck!" As it is, this note will have to do, although possibly I'll get to send you a teletype, too.

You will note that the ink seems to sink into this paper. That is because of the dampness in this tunnel where my office is located. The weather outside is hot and dry. You may be sure I

spend as little time as possible in this hole—but occasionally I
have to have conferences, etc. here. . . .

It's time to go see the Admiral. He's one of my best friends
—and a great fighting man. Good luck, and again, congratulations.

Devotedly,
Dad

*　　*　　*

". . . what is the use for us
old folks to come out . . . ?"

A Father in Communist China Writes a Son
Who Has Escaped:

In the winter of 1958–59, while Richard L. Walker was in the Far
East, he was given a collection of letters. "Some of these letters
have been sent through the open mail to Chinese relatives and
friends living abroad; others have been smuggled out. The letters
have been voluntarily handed over by Chinese who desired to
let the world know of the plight of their relatives and friends
under Communist rule," he has written. "Naturally, one condition
was fixed: that I safeguard my sources and delete any personal
names or other items which would aid in the identification of
the authors. . . . The letters themselves constitute the most effective possible presentation of the real meaning of the communes
in human terms." Below is one that speaks for itself:

Chin-chiang Hsien, Fukien Province
December 7, 1958

My Son:

Conditions here at home have changed tremendously. Now our village has been organized into a people's commune. Uncle's old house is now used as the public mess hall. The whole village is using it, getting their share of the meal from there.

Although we get our meals from the mess hall, actually we need to share the expenses for all if just to cook together. Therefore, I hope you will continue to send us some support.

Nobody would ever have known that the situation would change so much this year. Had we known this, would your mother have returned home from Hong Kong last year?

Although you want us to come out again, your son Ching-tsung just cannot get the permission to come out after repeated vain applications. Since he cannot come out, what is the use for us old folks to come out alone?

Ching-tsung is in senior primary, I know. But they spend all day for labor service and can only do some studying at night. He is lodging at school now and can only come home on Sundays. I cannot help feeling sad just thinking of it! If his mother were still alive, how could he still be here? I feel especially bad when thinking of the fact that he has already been to Hong Kong twice with your mother and could have stayed.

This time, the Government has required us to make a donation of 500 yuan and already has taken away 250 yuan which we borrowed from others. The Government is not satisfied as yet and is calling your mother for mobilization meetings every day.

Your Father

Certain lenience, accorded older people not capable of heavy work, sometimes made it possible to leave China, but the father who wrote this letter chose to stay in order to be near his grandson, a child in the fifth year of primary school and about twelve years old. "We are old like the setting sun," says another letter from parents who give the same address as that above. "We never thought the world would change as much as it has since last year. There is not much longer that we can see. Do the best you can. Do what your conscience tells you."

VI

* * *

The Light Touch

Is he witty, foolish, gay?
The child lives in the man . . .

Lord Burghley Dips His Pen in Dubious Rhyme:

William Cecil, Lord Burghley, principal secretary to three English sovereigns and the man Elizabeth I called her Alpha and Omega, was scarcely a poet, but his lack of talent did not deter him when he was moved to entertain his favorite daughter Ann. Following the sixteenth-century custom of giving presents on New Year's Day instead of on Christmas, Cecil decided in 1567 to accompany his gift with some advice disguised in execrable verse:

> As years do grow so cares increase
> And time will move to look to thrift,
> These years in me work nothing less
> Yet for your years and New Years gift
> To set you on work some thrift to feel
> I send you now a spinning wheel.
>
> But one thing first I wish and pray,
> Lest thirst of thrift might soon you tire,
> Only to spin one pound a day
> And play the rest as time require.
> Sweat not (O fy!), fling work in fire
> God send, who sendeth all thrift and wealth,
> You long years and your father health.

The recipient of this missive was ten at the time; three years later she was abortively betrothed to Sir Philip Sidney. When this engagement was broken, Ann spent the long years her father

wished her in a parentally arranged unhappy marriage with the
dissolute Earl of Oxford.

*   *   *

". . . as good for the father as the children . . ."

Sir Richard Steele Takes Pleasure in Conversing:

Charm runs through all the letters of the proprietor of the *Tatler*
and the *Spectator,* the periodicals that delighted the middle-brows
of Queen Anne's reign. Steele was an adoring husband and father,
who once wrote his wife that "you are to take this letter as
from your three best friends—Bess, Moll and Their Father." The
letter below is from Steele to Bess, who was four years older
than Molly.

7 October, 1720

My Dear Child,

I have yours of the 30th of last month; and, from your
diligence and improvement, conceive hopes of your being as
excellent a person as your mother: you have great opportunities
of becoming such a one, by observing the maxims and sentiments
of her bosom friend, Mrs. Keck, who has condescended to take
upon her the care of you and your sister, for which you are always to pay her the same respect as if she were your mother.

I have observed that your sister has, for the first time,
written the *initial* or first letters of her name. Tell her I am
highly delighted to see her subscription in such fair, and how

many fine things those two letters stand for when she writes them. M. S. is *milk* and *sugar*, *mirth* and *safety*, *music* and *songs*, *meat* and *sauce*, as well as *Molly* and *Spot*, and *Mary* and *Steele*.

You see I take pleasure in conversing with you, by prattling anything to divert you. I hope we shall next month have an happy meeting, when I shall entertain you with something that may be as good for the father as the children, and consequently please us. I am, Madam, your affectionate father, and most humble servant.

* * *

"What would life be without arithmetic . . . ?"

Sydney Smith Provides Parting Advice a Decade Before His Death:

Dickens once told a friend, "I wish you would tell Mr. Sydney Smith that of all the men I ever heard of and never saw, I have the greatest curiosity to see and the greatest interest to know him." Smith was, according to Byron, "the loudest wit I e'er was deafened with." He was "a fellow of infinite fun (if not much humour)" Thomas Carlyle said, and "a more profligate parson" than George IV would admit to having met. Whatever his contemporaries' judgment, he survives for his wit, which peppered his letters as well as his conversation. Lord Macaulay testified that Smith did not reserve his tongue's facility for his rich friends, but found his chief pleasure in keeping his wife and children in fits of laughter for hours on end. And when his children were not with him, Smith pursued them with his pen. He was a resident canon of St. Paul's when he composed this nosegay of a missive to his daughter Lucy.

London, 22 July, 1835

Lucy, Lucy, my dear child, don't tear your frock: tearing frocks is not in itself a proof of genius; but write as your mother writes, act as your mother acts; be frank, loyal, affectionate, simple, honest; and then integrity or laceration of frock is of little import.

And Lucy, dear child, mind your arithmetic. You know, in the first sum of yours I ever saw, there was a mistake. You had carried two (as a cab is licensed to do) and you ought, dear Lucy, to have carried but one. Is this a trifle? What would life be without arithmetic, but a scene of horrors?

You are going to Boulogne, the city of debts, peopled by men who never understood arithmetic; by the time you return, I shall probably have received my first paralytic stroke, and shall have lost all recollection of you; therefore I now give you my parting advice. Don't marry anybody who has not a tolerable understanding and a thousand a year, and God bless you, dear child!

There was a touch of the hypochondriac in Sydney Smith, but even that did not defeat his good humor. Having begun to suffer from gout when he wrote this letter, he described it as "the only enemy I do not wish to have at my feet." But though he expected the worst, he lived more than ten years after the "paralytic stroke" he forecast, and four years before his death he described to a friend his notion of the root of his physical problems: "Having ascertained the weight of what I could live upon, so as to preserve health and strength, and what I did live upon, I found that, between ten and seventy years of age, I had eaten and drunk forty four-horse wagon-loads of meat and drink more than would have preserved me in life and health. The value of this mass of nourishment I considered to be worth seven thousand pounds sterling. It occurred to me that I must, by my voracity, have starved to death fully a hundred persons. This is a frightful calculation, but irresistably true; and I think, dear Murray, your wagons would require an additional horse each!"

*   *   *

". . . I feel the pleasure I am giving
you more than you do."

Victor Hugo Describes His Travels to His Sons and Daughters:

Leopoldine, Charles, Francois-Victor and Adèle, the children of Victor Hugo, have been described as "living depositories for [their father's] sentimentality." Though Madame Hugo had an affair with Sainte-Beuve, and Hugo kept Juliette Drouet as his mistress for fifty years, the author was gushingly devoted to his family, and wrote them hundreds of letters whenever he was away from home. But this excessive emotion did nothing to stave off tragedy. His eldest daughter was drowned in the Seine soon after her marriage. Then, when Hugo had exiled himself to the island of Guernsey after the rise of Napoleon III, his family deserted him; his daughter Adèle ran away with an English officer. In 1839, however, basking in the adoration of the beautiful Juliette, Victor Hugo was full of himself and his talent for amusing his offspring:

Here are four sketches for you four, my Didine, I send *you* the Strasburg Cathedral to match that of Rheims; to Charlie, a view of a splendid old tower, surrounded by the sea, on the Island of Saint Honorat, two leagues from here (I have written the story of the tower at the side of the drawing); to Toto, the view of a suburb of Bâle, taken from the Cathedral Square; to Dédé, a few pretty Baden houses, with the town gate, I hope you will all be pleased with them, and then, when I get home, I will do some more sketches for those who have come off worst. I am the best off, after all, because I feel the pleasure I am giving you more than you do.

Those mountains behind the spire of Strasburg are the Black Forest.

This is a beautiful spot; I came to see the prison of the *Man with the Iron Mask.* I have also seen the Gulf Juan, where Napoleon landed in 1815. I start for Paris the day after to-morrow. I shall get there by the 18th or 19th. Kiss your dear good mother for me. Tell her I count on getting a letter from her at Châlon-sur-Saône. I had begun a long letter to her, but your drawings prevented me from finishing it. She will get it soon.

You are back at school again, Charlie. Work hard, be as good a scholar as you are a good boy, and love your father, who is always thinking of you.

I will enclose a letter for you in the next I write to your mother. Good-bye for the present, my darling Charlie.

We shall meet soon, my Toto. I have been at sea for the last fortnight. I have learned how to steer a sailing-boat to make plain knots, gasket knots, running knots, etc. I will show

you all my accomplishments in Paris. You are now at school;
you must work hard too, my pet.

My Dédé, I love you. You love Papa very much, don't
you? I wanted to pick some shells for you here; but I could not
find any. There is nothing but sand, which is ridiculous.

I am coming back to you, my Didine. Make your mother
happy, my darling, and love me. . . .

I embrace you all, my darlings.

Your father,

The drawings are all one inside the other. You must open
them very carefully.

*   *   *

"Nine years ago you were sent,
a sweet babe . . ."

The 'Father of *Little Women*' to the 'Mother of *Little Men*':

Of the four daughters of Bronson Alcott who served as the models
for *Little Women*, it was Anna who seemed most like him. Writing of her in his diary, he said, "Anna's profound intelligence, the
delicacy of her sentiment, the depth of her thoughts, her medita-
tion and ideal imagination are influences for Louisa's benefit."
It was Anna who persuaded Bronson to carry on after the failure
of his last experiment in communal living. She was the eldest
and—far more than Louisa, or even the self-sacrificing Mrs. Al-

cott—she had an intuitive faith in the theories that brought ridicule to her father during his lifetime, but have since been adopted by educators. On the morning of her ninth birthday, Anna found that Bronson had written her this note:

For Anna 1840

My dear Daughter:

With this morning's dawn opens a new year of your life on Earth. Nine years ago you were sent, a sweet babe, into this world, a joy and a hope to your father and mother. After a while, through many smiles and some few tears, you learned to lisp the name of father and mother and to make them feel how near and dear you were to their hearts whenever you pronounced their names. Now you are a still dearer object of love and hope to them as your soul buds and blossoms under their eyes. They watch the flower as it grows in the garden of life and beside its sisters, scents the air with its fragrance and delights the eye by its colors. Soon they will look not only for fragrance and beauty but for ripening and at last, ripe fruit also. May it be the fruit of goodness; may its leaves never wither: its flowers never fade: its fragrance never cease: but may it flourish in perpetual beauty and be transplanted in due time into the Garden of God, whose plants are green and bloom always: the amaranth of Heaven, the pride and care of angels. Thus speaks your father to you on this your birthmorn.

Anna was the first of the Alcott girls to marry and leave the tightly knit family. *Little Men* is based on the childhood of her sons.

✳   ✳   ✳

Thackeray Sends an Illustrated Report
of a Provincial Lecture:

Touring the English provinces in 1857 with a saucily entertaining lecture on the Hanoverian kings, William Makepeace Thackeray found boyish delight in describing his experiences to his almost-adult daughters. Many of his letters are illustrated, for throughout his life Thackeray continued to draw whatever caught his eye, underlining the absurdities of contemporary taste and manners.

Royal Hotel Sheffield
Chewsday. 17 Feb. [1857]

This comes rather late for Valentines day
—It is copied from 6 mugs in my sitting room
at the horrible inn at Halifax. This is a byooti-
ful Inn. I have the gayest parlour looking over
three smoky cheerful streets—a clean snug bed
room—a snug sleep—a pleasant book to read—
Colonel and Mrs. Forrest came to tea last night
after the lecture that's why I didn't write to

the girls. I liked them both, she pretty and
blonde, he very gentlemanlike. The people for the most part
didn't understand a word of the lecture. Old Fogy President
of Institution introduced me and insisted upon toddling into
the room with me on his arm. What, is Mr. Thackeray
infirm? asks Mrs. F. of her husband. It was Old Fogy
who was infirm. I had a very pleasant calm day at Fryston,
and yesterday for dinner here ate pheasant, one of a brace
which old Mr. Milnes insisted on sending to my daughters,
though I told him I wasn't going home. The last time I was at
F. in the year 41, Mrs. Milnes gave me a ribbon and a little
étui, a something for my children—they were little trots of small
size then—and she has been in Kingdom Come these 10 years
I believe.

I wish these horrible newspapers would leave my health
out. Some day the wolf will really come and no one will be
frightened. Keep off Wolf for a few months! I want to put
my lambs in comfortable shelter.

I am in the 4 vol. Mahon [a history of England]. It amuses
me. I have read Cockburn's *Memorials,* very pleasant too. it
is delightful weather and the skeei is blyew through the smoke.
Poor old Brookfield was born here my ♡ feels very soft
towards him. Do you smell anything in ♡ this ink? It was

thick, and I filled the bottle with brandy and soda-water. I have nothing to tell my dawlings but that I am very well busy and cheerful. I go to Leeds to lecture, and come back tonight to York. I like the quarters I am in. So you may go on directing to this Royal Hotel till Saturday. I mean you may send by Friday's post. I am glad you liked the drive to Q, never mind the ⅖.

Write to Granny and tell her how cheerfully your dear father writes and God bless my women says Papa.

Anne and Harriet Thackeray were never far from their father's thoughts. Six weeks after this letter, at a testimonial dinner given in his honor, he was almost overcome by emotion. His friend Dr. John Brown described the incident: "If you had seen his pathetic, dumb face, like a great child going to cry, when he stood up to return thanks for his Two Muses, his Daughters, you would have had a good honest cry. . . ."

*   *   *

". . . With the legs so long-like and the knees so short-like . . ."

Bret Harte Describes Some Customs of Europe to His Son:

In the summer of 1878, Bret Harte went to Europe for what was to be the rest of his life—serving first as consul at Crefield, Germany, and later in Glasgow. Though he never again lived with his family, he wrote scores of letters each year to his wife and children, among them his oldest son Frankie.

Crefield, January 18, 1879

My dear Frankie,

I had not time to answer your letter before, but you must never wait for that, but write to me as often as you can. It is the business of 'The Private Secretary' to write letters *to* as well as *for* the United States Consul.

It has been thus far a very cold, severe winter here. All the streams and ponds and *canals*—for the country here is flat, like Holland, and very low—have been frozen over, and even the banks of the Rhine, where it has overflowed, are glittering sheets of ice. As a consequence everybody is skating—except in this very business town of Crefield—men, women, and children. On Sunday last I noticed that the whole population of Düsseldorf seemed to be doing nothing else. Sunday in Catholic Germany, anyway, is always a holiday, and in Neuss and Linn the people bring their skates to church. Our large pond in the Hofgarten was reserved entirely for *sliding*. That is to say, about five hundred people were all sliding in rows—as New York boys do in the gutters.

You would be surprised at the sleds here, or, as they call them, 'Schlitten.' (By the way, a skate is a 'Schlittschuh,' literally a 'sled shoe,' and skating is 'Schlittschuhlaufen,' literally, 'to run on sled shoes.' The sled is made exactly like an armchair on runners, and in it they sit and are pulled or shoved from behind. Generally the boys or girls—one on each side— propel the sled forward—sometimes running, sometimes sliding, sometimes skating. The sleds are often very beautiful with carved gilt runners, like swans' necks, but I have never seen a sled like our American ones, on which I used to 'pony gutters' when I was a boy.

Germany is a great storehouse of toys, so you can imagine how interesting the shops were on Christmas. Papa could remember when the 'Private Secretary' and even his big brother 'Wodie' were both little boys and loved toys, and Papa, for their sakes, and partly because he was lonely, went into the shops. They were all very cheap, of course—so Papa bought a few for his Vice-Counsul's children and they cost him one mark and fifty pfennig—or about thirty-seven cents; and they made the children very happy. I sent you some of the New Year cards, which are half-toys, and are sent here to one's friends, like valentines.

Do you remember reading about the *stork* in the German story-books? I was greatly disappointed at not finding any here —but they are not in this part of Germany, and I did not see one until the other day, being just over the Dutch frontier, in a little village, I saw one perched on a chimney. While I was looking at it, three little children, scarcely older than Ethel, ran out and, taking hold of each other's little hands, began to sing to it. I was so much impressed by the simple childish words that I made them sing it again, for the promise of some pfennig to buy cakes—for German children are always ready for cakes. This is the song and I want you to teach it to Ethel. Remember that the words are pronounced exactly as they are spelt, and the letters, with the exception of the 'w's,' which are always pronounced like 'v's,' are the same as ours.

> 'Storch, Storch, Steiner!
> Mit den langen Beinen
> Und den kutz'n Knieen,

Jungfrau Marie hat ein Kind gefunden
War im geld gebunden.
Flieg über Beckerhaus, hol' drei Kecks heraus.
Mir einen, dir einen, und dem Andern auch einen!'

Perhaps I have not got it exactly right, I only trusted my ear. The English of it is:

'Stork, Stork, Steiner!'

'Steiner' is a children's word 'made up,' and means nothing.

'With the legs so long-like
And the knees so short-like,
Virgin Mary has a child found
That was in gold bound,
Fly over Baker's house
Bring three cakes to us,
One for me,
One for you,
And one for the other too!'

If you could have seen those little things swing their hands up, and scream at the top of their voices, in perfect trustfulness,

'Mir einen, dir einen, und dem Andern *auch* einen!' you'd have understood, as I did, all about German children, in an instant.

They believe storks bring good luck and always carry a baby in their bills as a present. Hence the allusion to the Virgin Mary.

Now begin this as your German lesson. Don't turn up your nose at it because it's childlike. Papa has begun to study German like a child, and has been in the third and fourth reader, and has broken his heart and worn his eyes out, over translation of 'Rothkäppchen'—('Little Red Riding Hood'), etc., etc.

But I must write no more to-day. God bless you, Frankie. Take good care of Mamma, and love your

Papa

*   *   *

"Treat her with more respect
than you do your venerable P. . . ."

T. H. Huxley Jests About the Departure of a Daughter:

Impish humor accents scores of the letters written by T. H. Huxley to his children. Though he described letter writing as the bête noire of his existence, he was a prodigious correspondent and a jolly one, often adorning his epistles with gay sketches. The letter which follows was written when his youngest daughter had left on a visit to her married sister.

4 Marlborough Place, N.W.
April 12, 1883

Dearest Pabelunza,—I was quite overcome to-day to find that you had vanished without a parting embrace to your "faded but fascinating" [3] parent. I clean forgot you were going to leave

---

[3] This was a family joke. A Dublin woman had been overheard to say, "Oh, there comes Professor Huxley—faded, but still fascinating."

this peaceful village for the whirl of Gloucester dissipation this morning—and the traces of weeping on your visage, which should have reminded me of our imminent parting, were absent.

My dear, I should like to have given you some good counsel. You are but a simple village maiden—don't be taken by the appearance of anybody. Consult your father—inclosing photograph and measurement (in inches)—in any case of difficulty.

Also give my love to the matron your sister, and tell her to look sharp after you. Treat her with more respect than you do your venerable P.—whose life will be gloom hidden by a film of heartless jests till you return.

Item.—Kisses to Ria and Co. [His grandchildren]—

Your desolated Pater.

*   *   *

". . . a faultless child, a perfect woman . . ."

Robert G. Ingersoll Celebrates the Birthday of a Daughter Who Is Thirty-Four:

Traveling thousands of miles a year as the most famous American lecturer of his times, Ingersoll wrote scores of letters to his daughters, almost invariably touching upon his unrestrained appreciation of his offspring. In the thirty-fourth birthday of his daughter

Eva, he found the occasion to say it all again, in a single lyrical paean.

Sept. 22nd, 1897

Dear Eva,

Thirty-four years of unbroken kindness, of cloudless sunshine, of perpetual joy, of constant love. Thirty-four years of happy smiles, of loving looks, of gentle words, of generous deeds. Thirty-four years of perfect days—perfect as the heart of June. Thirty-four years, a flower, a palm, a star; a faultless child, a perfect woman, wife and mother.

R. G. Ingersoll

*   *   *

". . . I've got to take a ride
on a grasshopper . . ."

O. Henry, in Prison, Writes in Jabberwocky to His Small Daughter:

Soon after the death of his wife, William Sydney Porter was sentenced to five years in prison on a charge of embezzlement, an affair that has never been cleared up. His eight-year-old daughter, Margaret, went to live with her maternal grandmother, who collaborated with O. Henry in obscuring the fact of his imprisonment. Below is the first letter he wrote to his little girl from the Ohio State Penitentiary.

Hello, Margaret:

Don't you remember me? I'm a Brownie, and my name is Aldibirontiphostiphornikophokos. If you see a star shoot and say my name seventeen times before it goes out, you will find a diamond ring in the track of the first blue cow's foot you see go down the road in a snowstorm while the red roses are blooming on the tomato vines. Try it some time. I know all about Anna and Arthur Dudley, but they don't see me. I was riding by on a squirrel the other day and saw you and Arthur Dudley give some fruit to some trainmen. Anna wouldn't come out. Well good-bye, I've got to take a ride on a grasshopper. I'll just sign my first letter—"A."

Margaret Porter was thirty before O. Henry told her the facts of his imprisonment, but he sent letters regularly during the three and a half years he spent as an Ohio convict. "Here it is summertime," he wrote shortly before his release, "and we haven't been fishing yet. Well, there's only one more month till July, and then we'll go, and no mistake."

*　　*　　*

Sir Edward Elgar Assures His Daughter Her Rabbits Are Well Fed:

Carice Elgar was fifteen when she was away from home as a guest of friends of her parents, and she had left her pets to be watched over by her composer father. Elgar had been knighted at Edward VII's coronation for which he wrote the official ode, and he maintained a dignified exterior for the world in general. But with his only child he was always merry. When she was a young woman he told her, "The country awaits your coming and so do I,—also a cask of cider which arrd yestere'en and the tapping thereof will be a sollum serremony between you & me!" The same intimate gaiety accents his account of events chosen to interest a fifteen-year-old:

Hereford
August 3, 1905

My dearest Chuck:

The animals are all well & *not* likely to remain so I fear, as everyone who goes by their house gives them something: I find the following *extras* were offered & devoured.

May [Carice's cousin]. 4 Chicory leaves each

Mother 2 large Carrots

Father 2 pea pods (full)

This happened in the evening: both Peter & Mopsy are lively & well after the treatment. The doves do not lend themselves to the stuffing so readily.

May & I escorted Mr Watkins to Withington & then went for a further ride: we 'struck' a bull in a field & he did not like us, or rather our bicycles which we were wheeling through the field: I made for once no suggestion as to 'waking him up'

243

—and he didn't want it. He woke us up, & we fled! Then a man came with a stake out of the hedge & kept him at bay while May & I discreetly withdrew.

I have no words for bulls.

Give my kind regards to Mr & Mrs Acworth [Carice's hosts]. I am glad you are enjoying your visit: it is raining heavily now & Mother is invited to a cricket tea!

Much love, yr affec father
Edward Elgar

Mr Atkins & May & I have put wire net on the backgarden gate *most beautifully* so you won't have to put boards for Peter &.

✳   ✳   ✳

"But one . . . combed the hair of the small boy!"

Theodore Roosevelt Reports a Hunting Incident:

When his children were too young to read, Roosevelt made a habit of sending them what they called "picture letters," illustrated with his own primitive but expressive drawings. He drew a bird feeding her young, or himself feeding an elk through a fence—or himself being serenaded by a jeering chorus of offspring singing "For he *is* a tyrant king." Below is a characteristic picture-letter addressed to a son while the President was on vacation.

244

Blessed Archie:

I just loved your letter. I was so glad to hear from you. I was afraid you would have trouble with your Latin. What a funny little fellow Opdyke must be; I am glad you like him. How do you get on in football?

We have found no bear. I shot a deer; I sent a picture of it to Kermit.

A small boy here caught several wildcats. When one was in the trap he would push a box towards it, and it would itself get into it, to hide; and so he would capture it alive. But one, instead of getting into the box, combed the hair of the small boy!

We have a great many hounds in camp; at night they gaze solemnly into the fire.

Dr. Lambert has caught a good many bass, which we have enjoyed at the camp table.

Shortly before he died, when helping to plan his *Letters to His Children,* edited by Joseph Bucklin Bishop, Roosevelt said, "I would rather have this book published than anything that has ever been written about me."

* * *

Otis Skinner Brightens the Path
for Cornelia Otis Skinner:

For any father whose vocation demands long absences from home, there is an extenuation of the normal problems with his growing children. For an actor, the problems may be even more accentuated. But for Otis Skinner who was a matinee idol—in the heyday of matinee idols—the plaudits and the absences were simply occupational hazards to be circumvented by letters. He was, certainly, as much a father on paper as most men succeed in being on the home premises. In the two letters that follow, there is more than a hint of his deep affinity for his daughter. Cornelia Otis Skinner says about the first message, "for the first time in my school career I had received a report card marked 'passing,' also I had started to study botany, a pleasant class because we were given window boxes in which to plant whatever we liked, my choice being the at least original combination of petunias and radishes."

My Accomplished Child:

It is very awful for your poor, ignorant, old father to realize that his daughter is so wondrous wise . . . that she has no failures in her report and that she knows all about botany and stamens and things.

Why, bless your heart! *I* don't know *anything* about botany. Isn't that a sad state to be in?

I climbed a mountain near here. I got so high (6100 feet above the sea) that the clouds were at my feet and I knew what it must be like to be an angel.

When I came down I met a snake stretched across the road . . . and he looked at me and I looked at him. And I said: "Mr.

Snake, you must die!" So I got some rocks and smashed him to *smithereens*. Do you know what *smithereens* are? I don't, but I *think* they look like baked beans. And Mr. Snake was over 5 feet long. . . . That's longer than you. And the joke is I don't know whether he was a *Mr.* Snake or *Mrs.* Snake.

When I come home, I shall eat nothing but radishes and shall wear petunias in my hair.

> Your loving
> Father

Not long before this letter, young Cornelia Skinner found that her more usual difficulties in coping with the hazards of scholarship had been complicated by illness. Her father, again on tour with his successful *The Honor of the Family,* was given an inkling of his daughter's problem by his wife. As a result, he wrote his child:

Beloved Person:

I did not know when I wrote and asked you about Hallowe'en that you were still in bed. If I had, I should not have been so mean.

I really don't know why we get sick at the wrong time. I really don't know why we get sick at all. If I could answer that mystery I should be as wise as God and it isn't given to any of us down on this earth to be as wise as that, is it? Perhaps when you grow up and become a nice velvet cheeked, snowy-haired, bright-eyed old lady you will know more about it. . . . I'm sure your dense-minded Daddy cannot tell . . . not now!

I remember I used to get sick at the wrong time. Once when the school term was coming to an end (and they *were* long terms when I was a kiddie) I was looking forward to the first day of my vacation because my mother had promised me I could go barefoot . . . and I *did* go barefoot. But I hadn't been without my shoes more than a few hours when I put my little heel on a cruel piece of slate and nearly tore it off. The doctor had to sew it up and I had to go to bed and stay there over two weeks. *And it was Vacation!* I don't think I should have minded so much if school term had still been on. (I'll tell you a secret . . . DON'T YOU TELL MOTHER!!) I was a dreadfully lazy scholar!

But you are coming out of your difficulties all right. You always do. You did last summer. You *finished well* after I had begun to think you were "all in." You first astonished me by doing your best work just before we reached the "Popa Kanzel" up from Latimar. And you walked down the Morteratsch Glacier like a soldier after that fearful tug up the sides and over the snowfields of the Diavolezza. But your greatest achievement was in the five or six miles of that stiff pull over the Bernina. When the village hove in sight, you led *me* a chase!

So you musn't be discouraged, but do as you always have done and you will find your joys will come in some other time. We always have just so much joy in our lives. We are like pitchers . . . we hold just so much: and sometimes we overflow and sometimes we are emptied out . . . and sometimes they take us and wash us out with soap because we have gotten dirty.

Well, dearie, this is a long letter for me to write you. Perhaps it is because I have lots of time in Louisville waiting for a train. Or perhaps it is because I love you very much.

Fajie

✳   ✳   ✳

Debussy Chats by Mail with His Eight-Year-Old Daughter:

Amid the furor caused by the première of *Pelléas et Millisande,* Claude Debussy met Emma Bardoc and fell in love. Each was married and each was forty-one, yet nothing could stop their romance, and in October, 1905, their daughter Chouchou was born. She was a love child, described by Gabriele d'Annunzio as "the freshest melody of Debussy's heart."

Saint-Petersbourg, Grand Hotel de l'Europe

11 December 1913

My dear little Chouchou,

Your poor papa is late in answering your lovely little letter. You should not hold it against him. . . . It is sad to be deprived for so many days of the pretty little face of Chouchou, to hear no more of your songs, your bursts of laughter, of all the noise, in fact, that makes you sometimes an insupportable little person, but most often a charming one.

What has become of M. Czerny, who has so much genius? Do you know:

this ballet air for fleas?

And old Xantho? Is he still as good? Does he still ruin the garden? I authorize you to scold him in a loud voice.

At the Koussevitskys in Moscow there are two charming bulldogs who have eyes like the frog that is in the salon (we are very good friends; I think that they would please you much), and a bird that sings almost as well as Miss Teyte.

All of this is indeed nice, but do not think that it is possible for me to be able to forget you for a second. On the contrary I think only of the day when I shall be with you again. In the meantime, think with tenderness of your old papa who embraces you a thousand times.

Claude DEBUSSY

Be very nice to your poor little mama; do all you can not to annoy her too much.

When her father died in 1918, little Chouchou wrote her half sister, "Papa is dead. These three words I don't understand, or I understand them too well. . . . And there I am, all alone, in battle against the indescribable grief of Mama." The following summer, not yet fourteen, Chouchou herself was dead.

*   *   *

"Try to know how we love you."

Richard Harding Davis Writes to His Nine-Month-Old Daughter:

The pioneer in the long line of American foreign correspondents was Richard Harding Davis, who reported wars throughout the world. In 1915, when he was on his way to the Ardennes front, he wrote this letter to his daughter Hope, who had been born the previous January.

251

My Dear Daughter:

So many weeks have passed since I saw you that by now you are able to read this without your mother looking over your shoulder and helping you with the big words. I have six sets of pictures of you. Every day I take them down and change them. Those your dear mother put in glass frames I do not change. Also, I have all the sweet fruits and chocolates and red bananas. How good of you to think of just the things your father likes. Some of them I gave to a little boy and girl. I play with them because soon my daughter will be as big. They have no mother like you, *of course;* they have no mother like *yours*—for except my mother there never was a mother like yours; so living, so tender, so unselfish and thoughtful. If she is reading this, kiss her for me. These little children have a father. He dresses them and bathes them himself. He is afraid of the cold; and sits in the sun; and coughs and shivers. His children and I play hide-and-seek, and, as you will know some day, for that game there is no such place as a steamer, with boats and ventilators and masts and alleyways. Some day we will play the game hiding behind the rocks and trees and rose bushes. Every day I watch the sun set, and know that you and your pretty mother are watching it, too. And all day I think of you both.

Be very good. Do not bump yourself. Do not eat matches. Do not play with scissors or cats. Do not forget your dad. Sleep when your mother wishes it. Love us both. Try to know how we love you. *That* you will never learn. Good-night and God keep you, and bless you.

Your Dad.

A month later, en route to Greece, Davis sketched a toy cat he carried with him as a present from his infant daughter:

SEE THE CAT!
HOPE GAVE THE CAT TO HER DAD.
IS THE CAT SAD?
YES
IS THE DAD SAD?
VERY!!
WHY IS THE CAT AND THE DAD SAD?
THEY WANT HOME AND HOPE.
DO THEY LOVE HOPE?
DON'T MAKE THEM LAUGH!

*   *   *

*". . . And now when you think it
isn't too much bother . . ."*

Ring Lardner Rhymes an Appeal for Mail from a Son in Paris:

Throughout his life Ring Lardner corresponded in verse—always playfully, but always, too, managing to say what he wanted to

253

say, whether it was chiding or hopeful. His oldest son, John, was nineteen and studying in Paris after a year at Harvard when the ailing Lardner, unable to sleep, left his bed to write a letter full of fondness and good spirits.

In New York
3 A.M. Sunday, Feb. 15, 1931
8 A.M. the same day in Paris

> The Vanderbilt Hotel
> Park Avenue at Thirty-fourth
> Street
> New York

Dear John——
Keep a hold of this letter
For fear you won't get anything better.
It is written in the "wee small" hours of the morning
Without an instant's warning;
I just suddenly took a notion,
Having sworn off the nightly self-administration of a sleeping
   potion,

To get out of bed and use my Underwood portable
Rather than go out and walk the streets and perhaps court a
   belle.
We are back from the South and stopping at the Hotel
   V-nde-b—t,
A place that some goose or gander built.
The food here would annoy you and pain you
More than that procurable in Pennsylvania,
And my opinion, which is seldom wrong,
Is that we won't be stopping here long.
If you should care to write us, through a sense of duty or pity,

Address us in care of the Bell Syndicate, 63 Park Row, N. Y.
    City,
Which, in association with the Chicago Tribune and New York
    Daily News,

Both of whom have plenty of money to lose,
Has engaged me to write a daily wire a la Will Rogers,
Designed to entertain young folks and old codgers.
I am supposed to write a hundred words or less per day
On timely topics, at pretty fair pay,
Though you are safe in betting
That I am not getting as much as Mr. Rogers is getting;
However, it keeps the wolf from the door
And while I may not be getting so much now, some day I may
    be getting more.

The reason I accepted this position
Was that my food was not giving me proper nutrition
And I seemed to lack the strength
To write short stories or plays or other works of any length.
When I am feeling fit again and everything is nice and tidy,
I intend to write the book of a musical show with a brand new
    idea.
A while ago I received a letter from a young man who, I am
    sure,
Had recently seen my own elegant signature,
And some time last autumn, ere the leaves were off the limb,
You had written my autograph and sent it to him;
He sent this autograph back and said he didn't want it;
By the vicious words of his accompanying letter I am still
    grieved and haunted.

David and your mother are in the next room,
Sleeping soundly, I trust, through the inexorable gloom.
The little one came in from school yesterday to meet us
And greet us with an advanced case of tonsilitis.
His throat is so sore that it irks him to swallow,
And if the ailment were to continue eight or ten years, his
    insides would become hollow.

Yesterday afternoon, your mother and I went to a matinee:
"America's Sweetheart," the new Fields, Rodgers and Hart
    musical play.

Gus Shy, John Sheehan, Jeanne Aubert and Ines Courtney are
    in it
And some of the songs are pretty enough to take home and play
    on your spinet;

In fact, it is the best Rodgers score I have heard for a long time
And I'll send you the three best numbers when I think it is song
    time.
I thought you very deftly and wittily
Described your visit to s—y Italy.
This spring, if you have another holiday,
I wish you would spend it in Montpellier
Where my mother's niece Amy Serre
Lives unless she has moved from there.
She is a widow about seventy and has a daughter
Who grew old before a suitor caughter.
But they are nice and the daughter is a musician
Who prefers playing the pianoforte to going fishing.
I shall find out whether they're still there, yes or no;

Meanwhile, you inform me whether you'd like to go.
At Miami Beach I saw very
Much of Paul Waner and Max Carey.
Paul is holding out for a much larger salary
And poor Max is about through playing for a baseball gallery.
He is a free agent and would make a swell coach;
Barney Dreyfuss would keep him if he (Barney) were not a
   roach.
"June Moon" closed in Boston a week ago
After making quite a lot of money for such a small show.
I still think they were rather silly
To let it play four weeks in Philly,
But we beat Holiday records in Detroit,
Greatly to the stockholders' delight.
My experience with "Smiles" is too funny and too long to put in
   a letter;
When I see you I can tell you better.
And now when you think it isn't too much bother
You might write a letter to sincerely your father.

Ring Lardner was very much a family man, and when he was able to be at home, he spent as much time with his children as possible. He helped them with their family newspaper, and encouraged them in creative writing. "Almost every family occasion was marked by a verse," Donald Elder writes in his biography, *Ring Lardner*.

To welcome their parents home from a trip, the children once wrote:

(To the tune of Yankee Doodle)
Daddy and Mother went away down south
Along with the Thornes and the Rices
And now they're coming home again
No matter what the price is

We're glad that they are at home once more
Because they made us lonesome
We hope that being with us again
Will make them stay at home some

* * *

". . . as all good and true rotarians should?"

James Joyce Merrily Chides His Son and Daughter-in-Law:

The famous decision of Judge John M. Woolsey had been made, and *Ulysses* had been published in the United States, when Joyce's son Giorgio, a singer, brought his wife and child to New York. There were many letters during this period, and they reflect Joyce's strong sense of family tie and its obligations. Above all, they show his sense of humor. "Even in his gloomiest letters," said his friend Stuart Gilbert, "the sudden glory of laughter was always breaking in." In the letter below, Joyce chides Giorgio and Helen for expecting a friend in Paris to move the furniture they had left behind.

Carleton Elite Hotel, Zürich
28 November 1934

Dear Oigroig and Neleh: Since everything's upside down I address you thusly. I have just spoken with Mrs. E. Jolas of Neuilly Seine who tells me she had such a nice long letter from you and that you have decided that she is to have the privilege of moving all the articles of furniture from the premises occupied by you in borough number given of the city of Paris. She was almost frantic with delight as she babbled over the telephone, breaking into snatches of gypsy music, yodelling, clacking her heels like Argentina and cracking her fingers. It is a perfect godsend for her. Poor Mrs. E. Jolas. For months and months she has been going around asking everybody to give her some sort of light work such as snuffing candles or putting salt in salt cellars, anything. But no one could help her. So she used to lie listlessly in a hammock all day and had begun to think there was no hope left. Now your wonderful letter has arrived and it has made her the happiest woman in all France today. She said to me 'Dearest J. Joyce, won't you give this little girl a great big hand?' and I replied 'Sure thing!' You know I come of a most musical family and there is nothing I enjoy so much as running up and down six flights of stairs with a cottage piano on my shoulders. The Paris-Orleans line has run an extension up to your door and is placing 2 powerful locomotives and fourteen trucks at your disposal. Mrs. E. J and myself will be as gleeful as two spoiled children. She will wear a white pinafore and a big blue sash and I cricket flannels. Have we cold feet about removals? No, sir! Do we put service before self as all good and true rotarians should? You have said it. So we're off at once.

> Goodbye, Zürich, I must leave you
> Though it breaks my head to [illegible]
> Something tells me I am needed
> In Paris to hump the beds.
> Bump! I hear the trunks a tumbling
> And I'm frantic for the fray

Farewell, *dolce far niente!*
Goodbye, Zürichsee!

This joking admonishment was written while Joyce faced the possibility of more legal trouble over *Ulysses*. It was not until three weeks later that he was able to write that the long debate was over: "In spite of the pressure of the puritan and Irish Catholic mob in the U. S. the Attorney General would not risk a third legal defeat in the Supreme Court. I won by default and the matter is at an end. Next, please."

Index

Account of Corsica (Boswell), 50

Adams, Charles Francis, 72

AE (George William Russell), 138

Albert, Prince, 62–64; *quoted,* 64; letters to his daughter, 63

Alcott, A. Bronson, 59–60, 231–32; letter to his daughters, 59; letter to Anna Alcott, 232; *quoted,* 60

Alcott, Anna, 60, 232; letter from her father, 232

Alcott, Louisa May, 59, 60; *quoted,* 59; letter from her father, 59

Anderson, John, xii, 136, 177–80; letter from his father, 177

Anderson, Robert, 132–36; letter from his father, 132

Anderson, Sherwood, xii, 132–36, 177–79; *quoted,* xii, 136, 177, 180; letters to his sons, 132, 177

Anne, Queen of England, 49

Annunzio, Gabriele d', 250

Appolinaris, 81–85; letter from his father, 81

Appolinaris Sidonius, 81–85; letter to his son, 81

Arblay, Alexandre d', 107–9

Arblay, Madam d' (Fanny Burney), 106–9; letter from her father, 107

Auchinleck, Alexander Boswel, Lord, 50–52; letter to his son, 51

Audubon, John James, 162–63; letters to his son, 163

Audubon, John Woodhouse, 163; letter from his father, 163

Audubon, Victor, 163

Bach, Johann-Sebastian, 165, 166

Bache, Richard, 53

Bache, Sarah (Franklin), 53

Bacon, Francis, xi

Baldwin, Stanley, 137

Bantock, Sir Granville, 137–39; letter to his son, 137

Bantock, Raymond, 137–39; letter from his father, 137

Bardoc, Emma, 250

Barrymore, Lionel, 33
Bauër, Henry, 58
Beethoven, Ludwig van, 216
Bloch, Ernest, 214–17; letter to his daughter, 214
Bloch, Suzanne, 214–17; letter from her father, 214
Booth, Evangeline, 206–9; letter from her father, 207
Booth, William, 206–9; letter to his daughter, 207
Bora, Catherine von, 5, 6
Boswell, James, 50–52; *quoted*, 52; letter from his father, 51
Bouchet, Mademoiselle de, 102
Boulanger, Nadia, 216
Brontë, Charlotte, 174
Brown, John, 193–96; letter to his children, 193
Browning, Elizabeth Barrett (Ba), 203
Browning, Robert, 203–5; *quoted*, 203; letter to his son, 203
Browning, Robert W., 203–5; letter from his father, 203
Bunau-Varilla, Philippe Jean, 206
Burghley, William Cecil, Lord, 225–26; letter to his daughter, 225
Burke, Edmund, 106
Burney, Charles, 106–9; letter to his daughter, 107
Burney, Fanny, *see* Arblay, Madame d'
Burroughs, John, 69–70; letter to his son, 69
Burroughs, Julian, 69–70; letter from his father, 69

Carlyle, Thomas, 227
Casson, Lewis, 139
Castiglione, Count Baldassare, letter to his children, 3–4.

Castiglione, Camillo, 4
Catherine the Great, 96–97; letter from her father, 96
Cecil, Ann, 225–26; letter from her father, 225
Cecilia (Burney), 109
Ceram, C. W., 168
Charles the Fair, king of France, 43–44
Charles I, king of England, xv, 91–95; letter to his son, 92
Charles II, king of England, xi, 48, 91–95; letter from his father, 92
Charles V, king of France, 4
Charles VIII, king of France, 162
Chasins, Abram, *quoted*, 33
Chesterfield, Philip Stanhope, Lord, 102–3; letter to his son, 102
Christian August, 96–97; letter to his daughter, Catherine the Great, 96
Churchill, Sir Winston, *quoted*, 88
Clare, Charles, 189–90; letter from his father, 190
Clare, John, 189–90; letter to his son, 190
Clemens, Clara, 70–71; letter from her father, 70
Clemens, Jean, death of, 70–71
Clemens, Samuel, *see* Twain, Mark
Cockburn, Henry Thomas, 234
Coleridge, Christabel, 17
Coleridge, Derwent, 14–17; letter from his father, 15
Coleridge, E. H., 17
Coleridge, Hartley, 14, 15, 17
Coleridge, Samuel Taylor, *quoted*, xiv, 14, 17; letter to Derwent Coleridge, 15
Coleridge, Sara, 15, 17
Cooper, James Fenimore, 191–92; letter to his daughter, 191
Cooper, Susan, 191–92; letter from her father, 191

Cromwell, Oliver, 46–48; letter to his son, 46

Cromwell, Richard, 46–48; letter from his father, 46

Curtis, Charles, 140

Davis, Richard Harding, 251–53; letters to his daughter, 252, 253

Debussy, Chouchou, 250–51; letter from her father, 250

Debussy, Claude, 250–51; letter to his daughter, 250

Despenser (Despencer), Hugh le, 44, 45

Dickens, Charles, xi–xii, 121–24, 227; quoted, xii, 123–24; letter to his son, 122

Dickens, Edward, 122–24; letter from his father, 122

Dickens, Henry, 124

Dickens, Mary, 123

Diderot, Denis, 98–102; letter to his daughter, 101; letter from his father, 98

Diderot père, 98–101; letter to his son, 98

Don Quixote de la Mancha (Cervantes), 101

Drouet, Juliette, 229

Dumas fils, 54–56, 58; letter from his father, 55

Dumas, Mme., see Ferrier, Ida

Dumas père, vii, 56–58; letter to his son, 55; to his daughter, 56

Eberstadt, Mrs. Frederick, 144–46; letter from her father, Ogden Nash, 144

Ecclesiastical Polity (Hooker), 92

Edward II, king of England, vii, 43–46; letter to his son, 43

Edward III, king of England, 43–46; letter from his father, 43

Edward IV, king of England, 88

Edward VII, king of England, 243

Eisenhower, Dwight D., 218–19; letter to his son, 218

Eisenhower, John, 218–19; letter from his father, 218

Elder, Donald, 257

Elgar, Sir Edward, 243–44; letter to his daughter, 243

Elizabeth, queen of George VI, 77

Elizabeth II, queen of England, 76–77; letter from her father, 76

Emerson, Edith, see Forbes, Mrs. William

Emerson, Ralph Waldo, 28, 30, 59; letter to his daughter, 65

Evalina (Burney), 106

Faerie Queen (Spenser), 92

Ferrier, Ida, 54, 55, 56

Fischer, Louis, 27, 30; quoted, 30

Fitzgerald, Frances Scott, xii, 35, 37; letter from her father, 35

Fitzgerald, F. Scott, xii, 35–37; quoted, xii, 37; letter to his daughter, 35

Forbes, Mrs. William, letter from her father, Ralph Waldo Emerson, 65

Fowler, William, 115–16

Fowler, Mrs. William, letter from her father, 115–16

Fox, Charles James, 106

Franklin, Benjamin, 52–54; letter to his daughter and son-in-law, 53

Frederick II, king of Prussia, 96

Frederick III, emperor of Germany, 62, 63, 64

Frend, Sophia, 112–14; letter from her father, 112

Frend, William, 112–14; letter to his daughter, 112

Furness, Horace Howard, 174–75; letter to his son, 174

Furness, H. H., Jr., 174–75; letter from his father, 174

Gabrilowitsch, Ossip, son-in-law of Mark Twain, 70, 71
Gandhi, Indira (Nehru), 31–33; *quoted*, 32–33; letter from her father, 31
Gandhi, Manilal, letter from his father, 28; *quoted*, 30
Gandhi, Mohandas K., 27–31; letter to his son, 28
Gauguin, Paul, 134
General William Booth Enters Into Heaven (Lindsay), 206–7
George IV, king of England, 227
George V, king of England, 130–31; letter to his son, 131
George VI, king of England, 76–77; letter to his daughter, 76
Gil Blas de Santillane (Le Sage), 101, 102
Gilbert, Stuart, English writer, 258
Godowsky, Dagmar, 33–34; *quoted*, 33
Godowsky, Leopold, 33–34; letter to his daughter, 34
Gods, Graves and Scholars (Ceram), 168
Goethe, Johann Wolfgang von, xi, 150, 167, 187–89; *quoted*, xi, 188; letter to his son, 188
Goethe, August von, 187–89; letter from his father, 188
Gonne, Maud, 137–38
Grant, U. S., 198
Gunther, John, 218

Händel, George Frederick, 165, 166
Hart, Lorenz, 256
Harte, Bret, 235–39; letter to his son, 236
Hauser, Arnold, *quoted*, 176

Hawthorne, Nathaniel, 70
Hay, John, 205–6; letter to his daughter, 205
Haydon, Benjamin Robert, *quoted*, 20
Hazlitt, Sarah Stoddart, 18
Hazlitt, William, 17–21, 116; letter to his son, 18
Hazlitt, William, 17–20; letter from his father, 18
Henry VI, king of England, 85, 86, 88
Henry VIII, king of England, 183
History of Music (Burney), 106
History of the World (Raleigh), 47
Hogarth, Georgina, 124
Hoover, Herbert, 140
Houston, Sam, 119–21; letter to his son, 119
Houston, Sam, Jr., 119–21; letter from his father, 119
Howells, William Dean, 70
Hugo, Victor, 229–31; letter to his children, 230
Huneker, James G., 33
Huxley, T. H., 239–41; letter to his daughter, 239

Idylls of the King (Tennyson), 64
Il Cortegiano (Castiglione), 3
Indian Opinion, 28, 30
Ingersoll, Robert G., 240–41; letter to his daughter, 241
Innocent VIII, Pope, 157
Isabella of France, consort of Edward II of England, 43–46

Jackson, Andrew, 21–22, 115; letter to his son, 21
Jackson, Andrew, Jr., 21–22; letter from his father, 21
James, Henry, 170–73; letter from his father, 170; *quoted*, 173

James, Henry, Sr., 170–73; letter to his son, 170

James, William, 22–25; letter to his daughter, 24

James, Margaret, letter from her father, 24

James I, king of Scotland and England, 88, 90

James II, king of England, 48–50; letter to his daughter, 49

Jane Eyre (Brontë), 174

Jarrell, Randall, *quoted*, 142

Jefferson, Martha, death of, 11, 13

Jefferson, Martha (Patsy) *see* Randolph, Martha

Jefferson, Thomas, 11–14, 35; letter to his daughter, 12; *quoted*, 11

Johnson, Dr. Samuel, xiv, 106; *quoted*, xiv

Jolas, Mrs. Eugene, 258–59

Joyce, James, 258–60; letter to his son and daughter-in-law, 258; *quoted*, 260

Julius II, Pope, 162

Juno and the Paycock (O'Casey), 138

Keyworth, Robert A., 37; letter to unborn child, 38

Knox, Philander Chase, 206

Koussevitzky, Serge, 250

Lafayette, Marquis de, 107

Lardner, John, 253–58; letter from his father, 254

Lardner, Ring, 253–58; letter to his son, 254

Leatherstocking Tales (Cooper), 191

Lee, Robert E., 197–98; letter to his son, 197

Lee, William H. Fitzhugh, 197–98; letter from his father, 197

Leo X, Pope, 157–62; letter from his father, 157

Libor Amoris (Hazlitt), 21

Lincoln, Abraham, 119, 206

Lindsay, Vachel, *quoted*, 207

Livingstone, David, xv, 124–30; letter to his son, 124; *quoted*, xv

Livingstone, Tom, 124–30; letter from his father, 124

London, Jack, xiv, 73–74; letter to his daughter, 74

London, Joan, xiv, 73–74; letter from her father, 74; *quoted*, xiv, 74

Loring, Katherine (Page), 71–73; letter from her father, Walter Hines Page, 72

Louis XIV, king of France, 141

Louis XV, king of France, 98, 100

Luther, Martin, letter to his son, 5–6

Macaulay, Thomas Babington, Baron, 227

McKinley, William, 26

Manon Lescaut (Prévost), 101

Margaret of Anjou, 85, 88

Mary, consort of William of Orange, 48–50; letter from her father, 49

Mary, queen of George V, 76

Mary, Queen of Scots, 88–89

Maule, Harry E., 37

Mayor, Richard, 47

Mazzini, Giuseppe, 28

Medici, Giovanni de', *see* Leo X, Pope

Medici, Lorenzo de', 157–62; letter to his son, 157

Memorials of His Time (Cockburn), 234

Mendelssohn, Abraham, 164–68; letter to his son, 164

Mendelssohn, Fanny, 165

Mendelssohn, Felix, 164–68; letter from his father, 164

Mendelssohn, Moses, Jewish philosopher, 164

Meredith, George, 66; letter to his daughter, 66

Meredith, Marie, letter from her father, 66

Millais, Sir John Everett, 203

Milnes, Richard Monckton (Baron Houghton), 234

Monet, Claude, 176

More, John, xiii, 184

More, Margaret, 183–84; letter from her father, 183

More, Sir Thomas, xii–xiv, 183–84; letter to his children, xii; letter to his daughter, 183; quoted, xiv

Mortimer, Roger, 43–46

Mozart, Leopold, 104–6; letter to his son, 104

Mozart, Wolfgang Amadeus, 104–6; letter from his father, 104

Murchison, Sir Roderick, 126

Napoleon I, 187, 230; quoted, 187

Napoleon III, 229

Nash, Isabel, see Eberstadt, Mrs. Frederick

Nash, Ogden, 144–46; letter to his daughter, 144

Nau, Jacques, 88–89

Nehru, Indira, see Gandhi, Indira

Nehru, Jawaharlal, 31–32; letter to his daughter, 31

Nelson, Edmund, 186–87; letter to his son, 186

Nelson, Horatio, Viscount, 186–87; letter from his father, 186

Obolenski, Prince Nikolai, 67, 68

O'Casey, Sean, 138

Page, Walter Hines, 71–73; letter to his daughter, 72

Pasteur, Louis, 198–99; letter to his children, 199; quoted, 199, 200

Patmore, Coventry, 116–18; letter from his father, 116

Patmore, P. G., 116–18; letter to his son, 116

Penn, William, letters from his father, 7, 8

Penn, William, the elder, letters to his son, 7, 8

Peter III, Czar, 96, 97

Philip, husband of Elizabeth II, 76, 77

Phillips, Wendell, 193

Pierrepont, Bess, 88–90; letter from her father, 89

Pierrepont, Sir Henry, 89–90; letter to his daughter, 89

Pissarro, Camille, 175–76; letter to his son, 175

Pissarro, Lucien, 175–76; letter from his father, 175

Pius XI, Pope, 184

Pliny the Younger, quoted, xiv

Pompadour, Marquise de, 100

Porter, Margaret, 241–42; letter from her father, 242

Porter, William Sydney (O. Henry), 241–42; letter to his daughter, 242

Raleigh, Sir Walter, English critic, xv

Raleigh, Sir Walter, 47, 90–91; letter to his son, 90; quoted, 91

Raleigh, Lady, 91

Raleigh, Walter, death of, 90, 91

Randolph, Martha (Jefferson), 11–14; letter from her father, 12; quoted, 13

Randolph, Thomas, 13–14

Renoir, Pierre Auguste, 176

Revere, Paul, 185; letter to his son, 185

Revere, Paul, Jr., letter from his father, 185

Ring Lardner (Elder), 257

Rodgers, Richard, 256

Rogers, Will, 255

Roosevelt, Archibald, 244–46; letter from his father, 245

Roosevelt, Theodore, 26, 71, 205, 244–46; *quoted*, 71; letters to his sons, 26, 245

Roosevelt, Gen. Theodore, letter from his father, 26–27

Root, Elihu, 206

Rousseau, Jean-Jacques, 100

Runyon, Damon, 146–50; letter to his son, 146

Runyon, Damon, Jr., 146–50; letter from his father, 146

Runyon, Mary, 147

Rural Hours (Cooper), 191–92

Ruskin, John, 28

Sacco, Dante, 209–14; letter from his father, 210

Sacco, Nicola, xiv, 209–14; *quoted*, xiv; letter to his son, 210

Sainte-Beuve, Charles Auguste, 229

Salzburg, Archbishop of, 104, 106

Schliemann, Heinrich, xv, 168–69; letter to his son, 168

Schliemann, Serge, 168–69; letter from his father, 168

Scott, Sir Walter, 110–11, 201; letter to his son, 110

Scott, Walter, 110–11; letter from his father, 110

Shaw, George Bernard, *quoted*, xvi

Sidney, Sir Philip, 225

Skinner, Cornelia Otis, 247–49; letters from her father, 247, 248

Skinner, Otis, 247–49; letters to his daughter, 247, 248

Smith, Lucy, 227–29; letter from her father, 228

Smith, Sydney, 227–29; letter to his daughter, 228

Social History of Art (Hauser), 176

Speaking of Pianists (Chasins), 33

Staël, Mme. de, 106

Stanhope, Eugenia, 103

Stanhope, Philip, 102–3; letter from his father, Lord Chesterfield, 102

Stanley, Henry M., 124, 130; *quoted*, 130

Steele, Sir Richard, 226–27; letter to his daughter, 226

Stein, Gertrude, 179

Stieglitz, Alfred, 179

Suffolk, John de la Pole, Duke of, 85–88; letter from his father, 86

Suffolk, William de la Pole, Duke of, xv, 85–88; *quoted*, xv; letter to his son, 86

Sussman, Mrs. S., letter from her father, xv; *quoted*, xvi

Table-Talk (Luther), *quoted*, 6

Tender Is the Night (Fitzgerald), 35

Tennyson, Alfred Lord, 64

Tête d'Or (Claudel), 139

Thackeray, Anne and Harriet, letter from their father, 233

Thackeray, William Makepeace, 233–35; letter to his daughters, 233

The Birth of Britain (Churchill), 88

The Book of War Letters (Maule), 37

The Death of Jean (Twain), 71

Theodoric II, 81

The Plough and the Stars (Synge), 138

The Viviparous Quadrupeds of North America (Audubon), 163

Thorndike, Sybil, 139

Tolstoy, Alexandra, *quoted*, 67

Tolstoy, Masha, 67–68; letter from her father, 68

Tolstoy, Leo, 30, 67–68, 70; *quoted*, 68; letter to his daughter, 68

Trollope, Anthony, 200–2; letters to his son, 201

Trollope, Henry M., 200–2; letters from his father, 201

Turgenev (Tourgenieff), Ivan, 170

Twain, Mark, 70–71; letter to his daughter, 70

Ulysses (Joyce), 258, 260

Upanishads, 28

Valentino, Rudolph, 33

Van Gogh, Vincent, 135

Vanzetti, Bartolomeo, 209–14

Verney, Edmund, 9–11; letters from his father, 9, 10

Verney, Sir Ralph, 9–11; letters to his son, 9, 10

Victoria, empress of Germany, 62–64; letters from her father, 63

Victoria, queen of England, 62, 64

Walker, Richard L., 219

Webster, Daniel, 61–62; letter to his son, 61

Webster, Fletcher, 61–62; letter from his father, 61

Webster, Harriet, *see* Fowler, Mrs. William

Webster, Noah, 114–16; *quoted*, 115; letter to his daughter, 115

White, William Allen, 140–41; letter to his son, 140

White, W. L., 140–41; letter from his father, 140

Whitney, Mrs. Payne, 205–6; letter from her father, John Hay, 205

William of Orange, king of England, 48–50

Williams, William Carlos, 142–44; letter to his son, 142

Williams, Dr. William E., letter from his father, 142

Windsor, Edward, Duke of, 130–31; letter from his father, 131

Winesburg, Ohio (Anderson), 132

Wise, James W., 75–76; letter from his father, 75

Wise, Stephen, 75–76; letter to his son, 75

Wolsey, Thomas, Cardinal, 183

Woolsey, John M., 258

Wordsworth, Dorothy, 14

Wordsworth, William, 14, 143

Yeats, W. B., 138

Young India, *quoted*, 27